THOUGHTS TO PONDER
NO. 2

DARING OBSERVATIONS ABOUT THE JEWISH TRADITION

Nathan Lopes Cardozo

URIM PUBLICATIONS
Jerusalem • New York

Thoughts to Ponder No. 2: Daring Observations About the Jewish Tradition
by Nathan Lopes Cardozo

Printed at Hemed Press, Israel. First Edition.

ISBN 965-7108-85-3

Urim Publications, P.O. Box 52287, Jerusalem 91521 Israel

Lambda Publishers Inc.
3709 13th Avenue Brooklyn, New York 11218 U.S.A.
Tel: 718-972-5449 Fax: 718-972-6307 mh@ejudaica.com

www.UrimPublications.com

"To be a Jew means to swim eternally against the dirty, criminal tide of man.

I am happy to belong to the most unhappy people on earth, for whom the Torah represents all that is most lofty and beautiful in law and morality."

–Emmanuel Levinas
"Difficult Freedom," *Essays on Judaism* (1977, p. 24)

CONTENTS

In memory of our father
Albert Russo, *a"h.*

In honor of our mother, Mary Russo.
May *Hashem* grant her a *refuah shelemah.*

Steve Russo and family

To my loving wife Sarah
who continues to enrich
all of our lives.
May your love of Jewish life be in your heart
and
continue to grow.

Peter Weintraub
Lauren and Ariela

❧

With thanks to our father Hilel Namvar
and mother Nosrat Namvar,
for the life and love they so devotedly granted
their children and grandchildren.

Sean and Nataly Namvar

In memory of our beloved and blessed leader,
torch and sage
Chacham Yedidia Shofet

Daniel and Melody Mahboubi

&

In memory of Abraham and Esther Hersh, *z"l*

Ronny and Toby Hersh

INTRODUCTION

This is the second volume of *Thoughts to Ponder*. Like the first volume, this book gives short insights into some often-neglected, misunderstood, and not-yet-discovered dimensions of Judaism. They are the fruits of my thoughts about God, the Torah, and the Jewish People, which I believe will throw new light on this great tradition.

Judaism defies definition. While some of us regret this and thus try to straightjacket our religion, I believe that autonomous thought is fundamental to appreciating Judaism properly, and that philosophical non-conformity is not only the right of every Jewish teacher, but his/her obligation. Students must understand that one can only comprehend the relevance of Judaism through ongoing existential personal discovery and struggle, and this can only be taught by example.

The Torah scroll has no vowels or cantillation marks. As such, the *ba'al koreh* – the Torah reader, guided by the tradition, must add his own breath to the words to make the text come to life. So too, we must make sure that Judaism, while remaining true to its essential teachings, encourages utter originality in every generation. Judaism must provide an antidote to the poisons of indolence, routine, callousness, and drifting with the current. It must dare and defy and be experienced as a perpetually new and ongoing event.

Like the first volume, this work is the result of weekly email correspondences I have had with colleagues, teachers, students, and friends over the last few years. The enthusiastic reception these insights received convinced me once more to make them available to a wider readership. I pray that these thoughts will inspire, and serve as starting points for deeper explorations into the vast sea of Jewish wisdom.

> Nathan Lopes Cardozo
> Jerusalem
> *Shevat* 5766 / January 2006

ACKNOWLEDGEMENTS

I am most thankful to my dear wife Frijda Regina Lopes Cardozo, my children, children in law and grandchildren for all the great support they give me teaching Torah and writing on Judaism.

My dear mother Bertha Lopes Cardozo, my brother Jacques Eduard Lopes Cardozo and family, and my mother in law Rosa Gnesin are a constant source of inspiration, together with Reverend and Mrs. Abraham Lopes Cardozo, New York and Mrs. Bep Spijer, The Hague.

Special thanks are due to Kam and Lily Babaoff, Los Angeles; David and Faranak Margolese, Jerusalem; Yosef and Leela Gitler, David and Barbara Brown, Raanana; Suny and Debby Sassoon, Los Angeles; Harry and Rachel Skydell, Rob and Elizabeth Kurtz, New York, Norman and Tzipora Pomeranz, Lauren and Ezra Kest, Los Angeles; Michael and Judith Kaiser, Toronto, and the American Board of the Cardozo School.

As always, many thanks to the staff of the David Cardozo Academy, Jerusalem: Rabbi Francis Nataf, Mr. Josh Halickman, and Mrs. Esther Peterman.

This book was edited by Jeanne Arenstein and by Mr. Jake Greenberg. Tzvi Mauer of Urim Publications was again willing to publish my work. To all of them, many thanks.

Finally my thanks to the *Ribon Ha'Olamim* for granting me the merit to teach and write about His Torah and creation.

Nathan Lopes Cardozo

The Dimensions of Prophecy and the Eternity of the Torah

The Torah uses several expressions for prophecy. Two phrases that appear frequently in this regard are, *Zeh Hadavar* – "This is the word," and *Koh Amar Hashem* – "Thus says God."

We find an example of the former in *Bamidbar* (30:2), where the Torah teaches the laws related to making vows. "And Moshe spoke to the heads of the tribes of the children of Israel and said, *'This is the word* that God has commanded: if a man makes a vow…'" An example of the latter occurs in *Shemot* (11:4). There Moshe informs the people that the promised redemption from the hardships of Egyptian slavery is imminent. *'Thus says the Lord*, 'About midnight I will go out into the midst of Egypt.'"

In response to this verse, Rashi comments as follows:

"Moshe prophesied with *'Koh Amar Hashem'* (Thus says God) and the prophets prophesied with *'Koh Amar Hashem.'* Moshe, however, added [another kind of prophecy] with the words, *'Zeh Hadavar'* (This is the word)."

Rabbi Eliyahu Mizrachi (1440–1525), in his classic commentary on Rashi, explains that this subtle difference in the language hints at the unique nature of Moshe's prophecy. The Talmud observes that with the exception of Moshe Rabeinu, the Jewish prophets experienced communication from God *be'aspaklaria she'ena me'ira* – via an obscured lens, which means that they only received prophecy while in trances or in dreams. Only Moshe received his prophecies at all times, even while fully conscious. He achieved a spiritual level on which nothing stood between him and God. Thus we say that Moshe's prophesy came to him *be'aspaklaria sheme'ira* – through an (absolutely) clear lens.

If this interpretation is correct, then the expression, *Koh amar Hashem* – "So says God," somehow implies a prophecy revealed through an "obscured lens." Commentators point out that this kind of prophecy does not have to be transmitted as a literal word-for-word repetition of the divine communication. *Koh Amar Hashem* actually means "This is *about* what God said," while *Zeh Hadavar* should be understood to mean, "This is the *exact* word."[1] In order to explain the Rashi commentary above (from which we learn that Moshe prophesied using both expressions) one could argue that before Moshe received the Torah, he prophesied on the level of all other prophets (*Koh Amar Hashem*), but that once he spoke with God "face to face" on Mt. Sinai, then he and his prophecy became elevated to a higher level, at which point he started to prophesize with *Zeh Hadavar.*

The Maharal, however, points out that we find instances in the Torah where Moshe prophesied with *Koh Amar* even *after* the revelation at Mt. Sinai – in which case, the earlier distinction can not be justified.[2] Consequently, the Maharal suggests another possible explanation for the two different prophetic expressions, which touches on the very nature of the Torah.

There are, in fact, two kinds of prophecy – one, of a temporary nature, and the other, eternal. The words Moshe uttered to inform the Israelites that God would lead them out of Egypt were very much contextual. They were specific to a certain time and place, and as such, *Koh Amar Hashem* sufficed. But when God reveals His will in the form of *mitzvot*, His message takes on an *eternal* stature, and therefore requires a more forceful phraseology: *Zeh Hadavar* – "*This* is the word [forever]."

The Maharal, with his usual profundity, explains that the first kind of prophecy portends a *change.* For example, in our case, in which Moshe tells the Israelites that God will effect a dramatic change by taking

---

[1] See, however, *Ha'emek Davar* of the Netziv, who rejects this interpretation (ad loc).

[2] *Gur Aryeh* (ad loc).

them out of Egypt. This was a *finite* affair belonging to the world of space and time, since change is only possible in a physical/temporal realm. The second variety of prophecy – the revelation of *mitzvot* – is, however, neither rooted in physicality nor in finitude. The *mitzvot* are the result of *eternal* spiritual realms touching the physical world without becoming part of it. As such, *mitzvot* have no existence or role in the physical world other than as an influence. Therefore, they manifest with *Zeh Hadavar* – "*This* is the unchanging, eternal word."

Because of this explanation, the Maharal can respond to one of the fundamental questions in Judaism. Why was God unwilling to give the Torah to the *Avot*, the Fathers, Avraham, Yitzchak and Yakov? If, indeed, the Torah contains such a profound message, why hold it back for so many generations?

With the above observations in hand, the matter becomes crystal clear. One cannot put something infinite and eternal into a finite vessel (obviously the vessel, no matter how strong, would shatter). As long as the Jewish people were merely a collection of individual mortals (even if those individuals possessed the towering stature and sterling character traits of Avraham, Yitzchak and Yakov), they could not receive an infinite Torah. Only after the Jews left Egypt and transformed into a chosen, religiously distinct nation – only after the Jewish people became an eternal entity – did they become a vessel capable of receiving God's eternal Torah.

Yosef: The Tragedy of Being a *Tzaddik*

When looking into the lives of the *Avot*, the three forefathers of the Jewish people, it is remarkable that not one of them officially earned the title of *"tzaddik"* – righteous man. The sages only gave Yosef, the son of Yakov, this high honor.[1] This is a rather strange phenomenon, as it cannot be denied that Avraham, Yitzchak and Yakov were outstandingly pious people, and generally acknowledged to be far greater (in the moral/spiritual dimension) than Yosef their heir.

Let us suggest that the reason the sages called only Yosef by this name, is because in many ways he did *not* appear, on the surface, to be a *tzaddik*.

During his reign in Egypt, the populace must have seen him as a somewhat ruthless ruler, who happily made the lives of his subjects unbearable when that suited his political agenda. We should never overlook the fact that the Torah and its commentaries offer us a huge advantage, telling us the whole story within a few chapters so that we never have time to think badly of Yosef before discovering his real intentions and the righteousness that motivated his seemingly cruel actions. This privileged perspective, however, was not available to most of the people with whom Yosef spent a good part of his life.

What must the common Egyptians have thought of Pharaoh's top advisor when he implemented a plan to buy all their possessions and enslave them? How their anger must have flared against him when he uprooted the entire population from their homes and relocated them to strange new areas throughout the country?[2] This was a massive program

---

[1] *Midrash Tanchuma* 58:4.

[2] *Bereishit* 47.

of population expulsion, which transformed the whole of Egypt into a refugee camp – a human tragedy of epic proportions.

Commentators explain that these drastic steps were necessary to revive the economy, save the country from even greater disasters, and set the stage for the Jewish people to dwell in the land. Still, few people in the country could have fathomed Yosef's agenda, and millions must have cursed his name for making their lives miserable.

Furthermore, Yosef's behavior towards his father and brothers superficially appears to be quite heartless. While ruling the land of Egypt, he never sent messengers to tell his father, Yakov, that he was still alive. How could Yosef allow his father, who loved him dearly, to live in constant anguish and mourning?[3]

Yosef's brothers and the servants in the palace no doubt thought that he was nothing more than a cruel and sadistic despot, psychologically tormenting his petitioners, and looking for ways to hurt them wherever possible. What else could they have concluded from his seemingly arbitrary decision to imprison Shimon and to thereby force the brothers to bring Benjamin to Egypt as the ransom?

Still, as many commentators explain, Yosef had no option but to do what he did.[4] How he must have longed to vindicate himself. Surely he dreamed of the day when he could reveal the truth – to let his family know his identity, and explain that it was his undying devotion to them that forced him to follow this seemingly harsh course of action.

Unfortunately, Yosef never got the opportunity to clear his name. His brothers continued to mistrust him, suspecting him of wanting revenge after the death of their father.[5] How painful it must have been

---

[3] For answers to this question see especially, Ramban and Abarbanel. For a general overview of the topic see also Rabbi B.S Jacobson, *Bina Bamikra*, Tel Aviv, 5713. English translation: *Meditations on the Torah*, Sinai Publishing, Tel Aviv, 1956.

[4] For further elucidation, see, among the many commentators, the observations of Ramban and Rabbi Samson Raphael Hirsch.

[5] *Bereishit* 60:50.

for Yosef to think that even in his old age none of his companions would ever know what his real intentions were![6]

The fact that he saved the Egyptian economy was little consolation, as the masses would not have understood the brilliance of his plan, nor would they necessarily have had the opportunity to enjoy its fruits. Their show of gratitude may well have been the kind of forced courtesy often paid to dictators.[7]

Indeed, this is the tragedy of nearly all *tzaddikim*, who by nature, generally can not reveal their real intentions or publicize the full extent of their righteousness. Often *tzaddikim* have to work under the most agonizing circumstances, even hurting people they love when that is what is required in order to prevent greater catastrophes. *Tzaddikim* hold themselves to a higher standard in order to achieve a higher purpose. But to stand for the truth, and to live by it without compromise does not always make a person popular with his peers, however noble his ultimate intentions.

These hidden *tzaddikim* do not work for the glory, but still, one would hope that their spiritual excellence would one day receive some manner of recognition. In most cases, however, there is little chance that such a turn of events will come to pass. This is the reason why the sages specifically bestowed Yosef with the title of *tzaddik*. While it is true that his father, grandfather, and great grandfather were men of gigantic spiritual and moral stature, only Yosef had to endure a double-life – a Machiavellian ruler in the public spotlight, and a holy-man completely hidden in obscurity – in order to achieve his God-given mission.

This is another aspect of the tragedy of being a *tzaddik*. To be righteous and to have one's deeds condemned, with the full awareness

---

[6] It is unclear whether he told his children. This depends on his reason for keeping his existence, identity, and whereabouts quiet from his father, brothers, and general populace. See the commentators mentioned in footnote above.

[7] *Bereishit* 47:25.

that perhaps nobody will ever know the real story, is one of the most painful human experiences. An authentic *tzaddik*, however, strives for the ultimate feeling of spiritual satisfaction that comes from the knowledge that the One Above knows the whole truth and is pleased with his deeds, as well as the unwavering conviction that it is more important to be a source of benefit to others than to be recognized or even understood.

The Sensitivity of the Torah and the Power of Language

When discussing the case of the *Eved Ivri* – the Hebrew Servant, the Torah states: "When you buy a Hebrew servant, six years he shall serve, and in the seventh year he shall go out into freedom for nothing."[1]

This situation only arises when the court convicts a Jew of theft and he is subsequently unable to make restitution. As a result, the thief must work as a servant to pay off his debt.[2]

A little later in the text, we read about a similar situation regarding a Hebrew maidservant: "And if a man sells his daughter to be a maidservant, she shall not go out as the man servants do."[3]

Both cases describe tragic circumstances; one in which a man has to sell himself into servitude because of a theft that he could not repay, and the other in which a father has to "sell" his young daughter out of sheer poverty, with the hope that she will survive and perhaps marry her new master or his son when she grows to maturity.

If one pays close attention to the wording of the text, one notices that the Torah uses the second person ("When *you* buy a servant...") in the *Eved Ivri* case, while the case of the Hebrew Maidservant is written in the third person ("And if *a man* sells *his* daughter...").

Why the difference in conjugation?

Meshivat Nefesh offers a profound explanation. According to the Talmudic Sages, buying a thief as a servant is a positive commandment, and was also a somewhat joyful occasion. The whole institution of servitude in Judaism is built on the premise that the time spent living and

---

[1] *Shemot* 21:1.
[2] Ibid., 22:2.
[3] Ibid., 21:7.

working in a proper Jewish home will help to rehabilitate the thief. Instead of going to jail to be surrounded by like-minded criminals, as is the procedure in other legal systems, he is adopted by a Jewish family who will try, throughout the 6 years of his servitude, to rebuild his self-respect and re-educate him by giving him a model of what life can be like. By taking him into the family and demonstrating how a proper family functions, the servant will develop (during his six year term) a new picture of what his future should look like. And at the end, he will leave with hope for enjoying a new and better way of life.

The most critical aspect of his education comes from the Torah's requirement that the members of the family treat him with the utmost respect. For example, if the family has only one pillow, Jewish law obligates the family to let the servant use it, since he must not be made to feel discriminated against by the family in even the slightest way.[4] The fact that he may not want to leave at the end of the six years is another proof of how well his new family must care for him.[5] Taking such a person under one's roof is, therefore, a happy occasion, and so the Torah speaks directly to the reader using the second person ("When *you* buy a Hebrew servant").

However, the case of the Hebrew maidservant is anything but happy. When a man's circumstances become so dire as to necessitate "selling" his daughter, however much he may be consoled by the monetary reward involved and/or the fact that the arrangement may give his daughter the opportunity for a better future, the situation remains, undeniably, a human tragedy. In that case, the Torah does not want to implicate the reader or relate to him as the case's sad protagonist in any way, and therefore does not use the second person, but rather creates a distance by speaking exclusively in the third person.

This extremely refined level of sensitivity, born from an unparalleled understanding of human psychology can only be found in

---

[4] See Maimonides, *Guide for the Perplexed*, 3:39.
[5] *Shemot* 21:5.

the Torah. No other legal system can compare – neither quantitatively, nor qualitatively.

Obviously, the details of the case are not the most striking feature of the Torah's instructions (we may even wonder if such a thing ever happened, given that Jewish law would require the community to help the father so that he would never be forced to sell his daughter). Rather, the way in which the Torah subtly conveys its wisdom regarding the way one should ideally communicate to his fellow man, demonstrates true Divinity. When a person speaks to his fellow man about something good, he should use the second person – "When *you* loan someone a million dollars..." But when one has to discuss a possible tragedy, one should speak in the third person: "When a man buries his relative...."

When a person lives by this advice, he demonstrates great sensitivity to the way words influence people's psychological states, as well as a desire to be a source of positive, growing energy for his fellow man.

– 4 –
The Courage to Admit a Mistake

It is so difficult to admit a mistake, yet nothing is so human as making one.

In *Bereishit*, we find a most powerful example of having the courage to admit an error – when Yakov's sons realized, at last, that they mistreated their brother Yosef when they sold him into slavery decades earlier.

After Yosef – now Pharaoh's top minister – put them in jail, they reassessed and admitted, "We are guilty about our brother, we saw the suffering of his soul when he pleaded to us, and we did not listen to him; therefore this misfortune has befallen us."[1]

To recognize and take responsibility for their mistake at this critical juncture was no simple matter. The brothers, as Rashi informs us, deliberated daily for years, questioning and critically evaluating their decision to send Yosef away by selling him to slave traders. Every day the brothers asked themselves if they acted correctly, and for years they concluded that indeed, justice was on their side.[2]

After more than 20 years the brothers were forced to view the situation from a different angle and suddenly realized that they had committed a horrible wrong against their own flesh and blood!

This must have been a devastating and traumatic experience the likes of which few of us would be psychologically strong enough to endure. Which man can openly declare that he has lived for decades in

---

[1] *Bereishit* 42:21.

[2] For several explanations of this story, see for example the essays by Nehama Leibowitz in *Studies in Bereishit (Genesis)*, World Zionist Organization, Department for Torah Education and Culture, Jerusalem, 1972.

sin? To admit that one made a mistake as the result of an impulsive decision is difficult enough, but to admit making a grave error after deliberating to the point where one was able to justify the act in his mind for years is, indeed, a most impressive feat.

Often, we make the tragic error of entrenching ourselves in our mistakes instead of admitting them, and, consequently, we deny ourselves the opportunity to get a fresh look at the issues involved. The mind can easily become a prisoner of our desires. To live well, one must make room for regret, so as to grow, change, and live afresh.

Ironically, most of us intuitively feel that admitting our mistakes will make us appear weak, and we fear that doing so will cause us to lose the respect of our fellow men. However, the Torah suggests that our intuition fails to reflect the reality in this case. We see that as long as the brothers insisted on their innocence, Yosef responded harshly, calling them spies and showing them little respect. By showing regret and openly admitting their mistake, they manifested true (human) greatness, at which point Yosef treated them with great compassion.

Looking into another, related lesson from the Torah, we see that Yitzchak Avinu, after discovering that he mistakenly gave his blessings to his younger son Yakov and not to his oldest son Esav, "trembled a great trembling."[3] Many people believe, incorrectly, that his realization that he blessed the wrong son made him tremble. The sages, however, explain that his extreme emotional response to this event came from the sudden epiphany that for years he had completely misinterpreted Esav's character, thinking that he was fit to be one of the fathers of the Jewish people.

Yitzchak "trembled a great trembling" because he was mistaken for years, with nearly disastrous consequences. It is remarkable that this error in judgment was seemingly more traumatic for Yitzchak than when his father Avraham informed him that he would be sacrificed on Mount

---

[3] *Bereishit* 27:33.

Moriah. Nowhere do we read that this news caused him even a modicum of trembling – let alone a "great trembling!"

In spite of the pain and anxiety, Yitzchak did not close his eyes or deny his mistake. Rather, he took full responsibility and corrected it as much as possible, and thus gave Esav only those blessings that truly applied to him.

So too, throughout the Talmud and later commentaries we see how the sages did not shy away from admitting a mistake. We find a famous case in point in Tractate *Shabbat* 63b:

"When Rabbi Dimi came he said in the name of Rabbi Yochanan, 'How do we know that woven material of whatever size is liable to become ritually unclean? From the Tzitz [the head plate worn by the High Priest].' Said Abaye to him, 'Was then the Tzitz woven? But it was taught: The Tzitz was a kind of golden plate, two fingers wide and it stretched around [the forehead] from ear to ear…' And Rabbi Eliezer son of Rabbi Yose said, 'I saw it in the city of Rome [where it was taken after the destruction of the Temple] and it was indeed made of gold.' When Rabbi Dimi went up to Nehardea he sent word, 'The things which I told you were erroneous.'"

Rabbi Dimi realized he was wrong and publicly admitted it. The importance of this admission is borne out by the fact that the Talmud felt it was worthwhile to record the interaction in its entirety.

This teaching – the importance of admitting one's mistakes – may well be the reason why even God sometimes seems to make "mistakes." In a famous passage in *Bava Metzia* (59b), we read that the sages decided a certain law against the opinion of Rabbi Eliezer who was known to be the sharpest mind of his day and whose opinions were fully supported by God:

"On that day Rabbi Eliezer brought every imaginable argument, but they (the sages) did not accept it. Said he to them: 'If the law is as I say, let this carob tree prove it.' Thereupon the carob tree was torn [miraculously] a hundred cubits out of its place – others say four hundred cubits. 'No proof can be brought from a carob tree,' they [the sages] retorted. Again he said to them, 'If the law is as I say, let this stream of water prove it.' Whereupon the stream of water flowed backwards. 'No proof can be brought from a stream of water,' they rejoined. Again he argued, 'If the law is as I say, let the walls of this schoolhouse prove it,' whereupon the walls inclined to fall. But Rabbi Yehoshua rebuked [the walls] and said, 'When scholars are engaged in a Halachic dispute, why should you interfere?' They did not fall, in honor of Rabbi Yehoshua. Nor did they return to their upright position, in honor of Rabbi Eliezer, and they are still standing thus inclined. Again he said to them, 'If the law is as I say, let it be proved from Heaven,' whereupon a Heavenly voice cried out, 'Why do you disagree with Rabbi Eliezer? In all matters the law is as he says!' But, Rabbi Yehoshua arose and exclaimed, 'It [the law] is not in Heaven."

What did he mean by this? Said Rabbi Yermiyahu: 'It means that the Torah has already been given at Mount Sinai, so we no longer pay any attention to Heavenly voices, because You, God, wrote long ago in the Torah at Mount Sinai, 'After the majority one must incline.'"[4]

This remarkable story raises many questions: Why did God send a voice in support of Rabbi Eliezer? Why did He not agree with Rabbi Yehoshua? Does the Torah not clearly state that in cases of rabbinic conflict, the law goes according to the majority opinion? Why did He deliberately try to confuse the sages by giving His opinion against the prior principle that He set forth at Sinai?

Perhaps God wanted to appear to make a "mistake!" This interpretation reads well from the continuation of the story:

"Rabbi Nathan met Eliyahu [the prophet, who is considered to be immortal] and asked him, 'What did the Holy One, blessed be He, do at that moment [when Rabbi Yehoshua declared that he would not obey His heavenly voice]? He replied, 'He laughed, saying, 'My sons have defeated Me, My sons have defeated Me!'"

---

[4] *Shemot* 23:2.

If God, the ultimate Source of wisdom, went out of His way to "make a mistake" so that He could then publicize His admission, we can be well-assured that to own up to our errors is the most honorable way to deal with them. Instead of feeling insecure and fearing for our reputations, we should know that taking full responsibility will only increase our dignity in the eyes of our peers. Indeed, to err is human, and to admit it is Divine.

The Tabernacle and Bach's Compositions

When studying the last chapters of *Shemot* (Exodus), one should be puzzled by the great attention to detail and the repetition of the architectural instructions for building the *Mishkan* (Tabernacle). While the Torah is normally very taciturn with its words, here we find an overflow of seemingly redundant messages and an unusual emphasis on minutiae. Not even the smallest nuance (the Torah literally mentions each pin and string!) is left to the imagination.

This pedantic approach comes as a real surprise in light of the spiritual state of mind the Israelites must have achieved in order to help erect the *Mishkan*. This required personal input, creativity, and a great deal of inspiration which could only come from the depths of the human heart. This is a paradox, as the human ingredients in this most exalted structure could not be restricted by such fastidious rules and precise measurements.

The Torah's micro-management of this design project would also seem to contradict the very purpose of the structure. The Mishkan's primary function, like that of Solomon's Temple in Jerusalem many years later, was to be the central locus of Divine worship for the Jewish people, and a source of constant inspiration. It was a space designed to fill the hearts of men with a spirit of religious ecstasy and devotion. In fact, many who visited the Mishkan or the Temple, were entirely transformed by the experience.[1]

Furthermore, the Torah informs us that a Jew should be "urged by his heart" to help build the Mishkan and to contribute in a spontaneous way to its upkeep.

---

[1] See *Pirkei Avot* 5:8.

How do we reconcile these contradictions? Formality versus spontaneity; total commitment to the letter of the law versus unprecedented outbursts of emotion and religious devotion. Are these not mutually exclusive and irreconcilable?

It is here that the study of music becomes of vital interest. Let us recall an earlier observation concerning the great composer, Johann Sebastian Bach (1685–1750).[2] In his music we find an expression of a similar paradox, in which strict adherence to rigid rules of composition somehow gives birth to phenomenal outbursts of emotion. In Bach's works, more than in any other composer's, we find a great amount of repetition, as well as almost mathematical patterns, combined with a seemingly limitless creativity. The overall effect is one of staggering genius.

Martin van Amerongen, Dutch author and music critic, writes in his book, *His Lightening, His Thunder: About the St. Matthew Passion*, "When one hears Bach's music, it feels like being struck by an uppercut under the chin and staying unconscious for the rest of the day. Bach is the man of the iron fist, of the controlled emotions, who, notwithstanding this, shows great personal passion." When Bach played the music himself (harpsichord), he was able to keep an eye on seven diverse musical patterns simultaneously, correct them and write variations on them without ever violating the rules of the traditional music of his day.

Within this combination of unyielding commitment to detail, accuracy and skill, there is the danger that one may fall into a kind of routine and lose out on the "real" music behind the notes. Indeed, this is the worry of every conductor and orchestra. However, one is able to prevent this by going back to the original text and its score. There, no matter how many times one has seen the piece before, one can discover new perspectives that recreate and redefine the whole composition without altering an iota.

---

[2] See *Thoughts to Ponder No. 1*, Chapter 28.

We would suggest that the reason for this wonderful occurrence is that since the mathematical precision does not allow for any horizontal expansion, the composer must channel his creative talents vertically, to give depth to whatever lies within the confines of the structure. Instead of merely perusing the vast surface area, the composer is, like an archeologist, forced to go to rock-bottom in search of all the hidden possibilities, and to exert himself in order to unearth them.

This, we maintain, is the genius of the Mishkan, and with this understanding we can solve the paradox of its architectural precision and the need for genuine religious passion.

When listening to the nearly endless repetitions of musical themes in Bach's compositions, his genius is revealed in the subtle variations – one more note or one more instrument – by which a familiar musical pattern becomes transformed into something that sounds totally different and evokes an entirely new set of emotions.

So too, a person who worshipped in the Mishkan did not go to experience a great quantity of religious "notes," but an unprecedented quality found in every pin and string, which would uplift his spirits. Every structural repetition added another dimension depending on the context in which it appeared and the slight variations that accompanied it.[3]

Just like every keen listener of Bach's compositions, every visitor of the Tabernacle was "knocked unconscious" – i.e., underwent a radical transformation – by his meditations on the depths inherent in every subtle detail, and from feeling their religious vibrations.

---

[3] For a full understanding of the religious and inspirational meaning of all the items in the *Mishkan* see especially the commentaries of Don Yitzchak Abarvanel (1437–1508) and Rabbi Samson Raphael Hirsch, (1808–1888) on *Vayikra* (Leviticus).

6

A "Brenn" or "Familiarity Breeds Contempt"

A Chassidic Rebbe was once asked: "If you could save one thing from your burning home, what would it be?" "The fire," answered the Rebbe, "because it is the *brenn*[1] which makes life worth living." Indeed, life becomes meaningful and thus worth living, only when man's soul "burns from within" for his ideals and his life's purpose. The art is to live each moment as new, as unique, as a challenge, and as an encounter with the Divine.

When carefully reading the 46th chapter in the book of Yechezkel, we read a most revealing instruction concerning the common people who visit the Temple on the festivals:

"And on the *mo'adim* (festivals) when the common people come before the Lord, whoever enters the north gate to bow low shall leave by the south gate, and whoever enters by the south gate shall leave by the north gate. They shall not go back through the gate by which they came, but they shall go out through the opposite one."[2]

What difference could it possibly make whether one leaves through the north or south gate?

Rabbi Yonathan Eybeschuetz, 18th century author of the classic *Ya'aroth Devash,* provides a most profound explanation for this seemingly bizarre command: "God was particular that they should not see the same gate twice, lest they see the Temple gate like they see the gates of their homes."

---

[1] *Brenn* is a German-Yiddish expression for an emotional inner-fire in the heart of man.

[2] Verse nine.

The prohibition of leaving the Temple via the same route one entered, was instituted in order that no one would get accustomed and desensitized to the Temple's environment by seeing it twice *from the same point of view*. Nothing is more dangerous than getting used to one's surroundings. As the saying goes: "Familiarity breeds contempt." This indeed is the essence of proper religious life – to avoid complacency and to make sure that one remains astonished and amazed by life.

To appreciate life requires a special kind of mindset. One must cultivate the ability to see things differently, to reframe, to change perspectives, sometimes to turn a thing upside down. This is one of the great blessings of religion. Most of the time religious insight does not reveal something entirely new, but rather calls attentions to those things one has seen before but never properly noticed.

Western culture offers a very limited and selective view of life. In fact it completely ignores much of what is most beautiful, rendering them invisible, and thereby making it extremely difficult to enjoy life fully and to feel the exhilaration of existence. Religion is a protest against this narrow-mindedness that takes so much for granted, allowing for deep meditation on the wondrousness inherent in the most simple events. Religion transforms the obvious and mundane into the mysterious and mystical. Ludwig Wittgenstein, the great Austrian philosopher remarked that, "Not *how* the world is, but *that* it is, is the mystical." Not *how* we are, but *that* we are is cause for unceasing wonder.

> *To see the world in a grain of sand*
> *And heaven in a wild flower*
> *Hold infinity in the palm of your hand,*
> *And eternity in an hour*
> –William Blake, "Auguries of Innocence"

The raison d'être of the Temple was to give man an opportunity to see and understand the world from an entirely different perspective. The symbolism of its construction and the vessels found within forced men to wake up from their secular ideologies and see the world's divine metaphysical dimensions. To underscore this fact, and to ensure the success of the Temple's purpose, the common people were not allowed to see one gate twice during a single visit, lest they fail to internalize the Temple's message...lest they continue to live their lives without an inner *brenn*.

7

Revolution Through a Single Word

When studying the life of Avraham, we often wonder what about him was so special that he became the first "Jew" in all of history. As the progenitor of Judaism he laid the foundations of the western world's entire body of religious thought.[1] Not only did Judaism give birth to two other world religions, Christianity and Islam, but it also became the root source of the modern world's legal systems and its concepts of justice and morality. What was Avraham's secret?

Conventional wisdom on the subject puts forth the notion that Avraham "discovered" God after mankind had fallen prey to idol worship, and that *this* was his main contribution to the world. This however, cannot be the whole story. It is clear from the Torah that many other individuals also recognized God as their object of worship. We read, for example, that Avimelech, King of Gerar, and Melchizedek, King of Salem, believed in God even before they met Avraham.[2] More importantly though, introducing the world to monotheism without also offering a way of life that allows a person to forge a connection to the one and only God, without morality and justice, does not seem like such a revolutionary breakthrough. If this was Avraham's contribution, and no more, how did he manage to capture the hearts and minds of the entire western world?

Rabbi Moshe Avigdor Amiel (1883–1946) *z"l*, former Chief Rabbi of Tel Aviv, suggested that Avraham became the father of all

---

[1] There are some who suggest that Avraham's ideas reached the Orient through the sons he sent to the East with "gifts" and thus he may have influenced the development of Eastern spiritual practices as well.

[2] *Bereishit* 14.

western religions, justice, and morality by replacing a single word.[3] And it was this semantic change that set humanity on a new course for the rest of history.

When Adam first meets his wife Chava (after God formed her from Adam's rib), he identifies her with the words: "This now is the bone of my bones and the flesh of my flesh."[4] This statement strikes us as slightly odd, since we would have expected a person on the level of Adam to speak about his soul mate in spiritual terms, rather than make reference to her physical constitution. This is even more startling when we consider that they had not yet eaten from the tree of knowledge of good and evil, and as such lived on an extremely rarified plane of existence within the Garden of Eden.

During the following centuries we see many times that human beings continued to see themselves in terms of *flesh*. Even the Torah, which originally called man a "nefesh chaya" – a living, speaking being,[5] also describes man in terms of his flesh. We see this most clearly in the story of Noach and the flood.

"And God saw the earth and behold, it was corrupt, for all flesh had corrupted their way upon the earth."[6]

However, once Avraham enters the Biblical narrative, man is never again described as flesh. From this moment onwards, mankind once more becomes elevated to the level of soul – *nefesh.*[7]

This strongly suggests that Avraham's most important contribution to the world was not so much the discovery of God, but rather the transmission of the message that the human being is more soul than flesh. By teaching mankind to think of himself as a *nefesh*, rather than just another form of *flesh*, Avraham laid the foundations of morality and

---

[3] *LeNevuchei le-Tekufa*, 1928.
[4] *Bereishit* 2:23.
[5] *Bereishit* 2:7.
[6] *Bereishit* 6:12.
[7] See for example *Bereishit* 12:13.

simultaneously pushed the role of religion into entirely new realms. Where religion previously functioned merely to make people aware of the one, true God's existence, now it would also serve to make man aware of his soul, and that as a moral being he is responsible for his actions.

We see how Avraham managed to inspire even the most depraved characters to change their language from physical to spiritual in an episode involving the King of Sedom. After Avraham rescued Lot in the context of a much bigger war, the King of Sedom says, "Give me the *souls* and take the goods for yourself."[8]

One must merely consider the abominable practices associated with the ancient pagan cults or Plato's criticism of the Greek's polytheistic religion and the great moral evils it bred, to realize that religion and morality do not always go hand-in-hand.[9] With the advent of Judaism, however, the world was introduced to the idea that religion and ethical living are inseparable, because when man is seen in terms of soul, then he can be asked to behave in an ethical manner (because soul implies existence beyond the physical). Once man discovers who he really is, then values such as "kedusha" (holiness) and "tahara" (spiritual purity) become relevant realities.

This weltanshauung infiltrated western civilization as a result of Avraham's revolution – when he replaced the word *flesh* in mankind's understanding of self, with the word *soul.*

---

[8] *Bereishit* 13:21.
[9] *The Republic*, 111, pp. 250–1, Jowett's translation.

Universal Love – Is it Possible?

In a world filled with animosity, the concept of Universal Love has become a widely discussed ideal in popular culture. Many believe that when all men love each other equally, then all the world's problems will be solved and world peace will inevitably ensue. The logical implication of this view is that discrimination of any kind, whereby a person loves some people more than others, is the cause of poverty, hatred, jealousy, and war.

To support this philosophy, its advocates like to point out that the Bible shares their view. The famous verse from *Vayikra* (19:18) that teaches us to "love our neighbor as we love ourselves" is frequently quoted by those convinced that all we need is universal love.

It is therefore most remarkable that the Talmud records a story that seems to challenge even the possibility of ever loving all men equally. In *Bava Metzia* (62a) the Talmud relates the story of two people who find themselves in a desert far removed from civilization. Tragically, only one of them has a canteen filled with water, and they realize that if they divide the water, both will die. If the canteen's owner keeps all the water for himself, however, then he will likely survive. What to do? Based on the principle of universal and equal love, would it not be the righteous choice to share the water and die together as brothers? Indeed this is the opinion of a scholar by the name of Ben Petura. Nothing demonstrates our love for our fellow man more than dying with him.

Somewhat surprising, however, is the fact that Ben Petura's position is opposed by one of the greatest sages of all time: Rabbi Akiva. The latter takes issue and insists that the moral course of action calls for the owner of the container to drink *all* the water! Surely he is obliged to do everything he can to save his neighbor's life, but this responsibility only comes to bear *after* he has guaranteed his own survival.

According to Rabbi Akiva this is not a suggestion for the common man, which the really pious may ignore so as to prove their limitless love for their fellow men. Rather it is God's sacrosanct law and may never be violated. In light of this episode, it is most notable that Rabbi Akiva, in another section of the Oral Tradition, teaches that the law of loving one's neighbor as oneself is "the Torah's most fundamental principle!"[1]

How could Rabbi Akiva rule that the canteen owner should keep the water for himself and let his fellow die of thirst, and also hold that brotherly love is the ultimate principle of God's law? Do these ideas not directly contradict each other? After all, the verse says clearly to love one's neighbor as much as one loves oneself!

Rabbi Akiva's position becomes tenable once we recognize that he read the verse differently. Unlike Ben Petura, he did not believe that a human being could ever love another person as much as he loves himself. Self preservation is the core of human existence. Indeed, it is impossible to love someone else without at the very least, being alive! So then self-love is the place from which all other love can emerge and grow, and this is indeed what the verse suggests. The biblical text does not read, *Ve'ahavta re'acha kamocha* – Love your neighbor like yourself. Rather it says, *Ve'ahavta LE-re'acha kamocha* – Love *towards* your neighbor as much as you love yourself.

This means that one does not need to love one's neighbor exactly as much as he loves himself, but that one should wish for his fellow men all the good things that he wishes for himself.[2] The notion of loving all people equally is a farce and a destructive one at that. What would be of a man who professed to his wife, "My darling, I love you. I love you *so* much. I love you as much as I love...that other woman sitting in her

---

[1] Jerusalem Talmud, *Nedarim* 9:4.
[2] See Ramban and R. Samson Rafael Hirsch, ad loc.

40

garden across the street. And also that lovely girl riding her bike. In fact, I love you as much as I love all the women who I never met... I love you as much as I love everyone else on the planet?"[3]

We live for love. We are prepared to give up almost anything to experience a deep and loving relationship. But we should not allow ourselves to get confused, and to think that love does not necessarily imply preference. Real love makes distinctions. A man loves a woman because she is special in his eyes. And this feeling of recognizing another person's uniqueness and inherent greatness is one of the most beautiful things that can ever befall a human being. This discriminating love can motivate and energize us in ways that nothing else can. It gets us out of our beds in the morning, makes us feel warm and tingly inside, causes us to attempt heroic feats, pushes us to make sacrifices, and spurs us to demonstrate divine levels of loyalty. Whoever thinks that one should love all people equally has no idea what love is about and will not ever truly love even a single person.

Two men who attempted to create a world of universal love were Stalin and Mao. The societies they designed forced people to dress the same, eat the same, talk the same and think the same. It was a loveless world without warmth and joy, and it invited total disaster. This mistaken philosophy is also espoused by the followers of Hare Krishna and a number of similar Eastern religious systems, as well as by Christians.

Obviously one must show respect to all people and try to take care of their needs as much as possible, but to believe that the world would get any better by eliminating the notion of special love for special people is a most horrific miscalculation. Our world would be much better

---

[3] See *Imagine: On Love and Lennon* by Ze'ev Maghen, *Azure*, Spring 1999.

served by people realizing the truth of Rabbi Akiva's interpretation, and doing their best just to love even one person well and truly.[4]

---

[4] Ben Petura's view definitely does not represent the authentic Jewish outlook on life and love, and in fact reminds us of the Christian interpretation of love which claims to be universal. It therefore does not come as a complete surprise that some scholars have expressed the opinion that Ben Petura is in fact a corruption of the name Ben Pandora or Ben Pantera. Pandora or Pantera is the name of Joseph, the father of Jesus (See *Targum* 11 on the scroll of Esther). If that is true then Ben Petura is Jesus himself (See also *Tosefta Chullin* 11:22, 24). In that case it seems the Talmud states both opinions in order to contradict early Christian interpretations of the Torah.

9

Song and Ecstasy in the Religious Experience[1]

"Now, Write This Song for Yourselves and Teach it to the Children of Israel" (*Devarim* 31:19). With this verse God commands Moshe to write down the words of the Torah, and to teach the Children of Israel to contemplate them and use them as their guide. Commentators and philosophers throughout the ages have wondered why the contents of this instruction manual should be called a *song?*

Just after Moshe's death and before the battle at Jericho, a heavenly being with the appearance of a man confronts Yehoshua, the Jewish people's new leader, approaching him a sword in his hand. Yehoshua asks him, "*HaLanu Ata?*" Are you with us [or against us]?" And this divine being responds, "No, I am the commander of God's legion. Now I have come!" *And Yehoshua prostrated himself before him...*[2]

The Talmud interprets this rather strange and incomprehensible interaction as an allegory whereby Yehoshua understood the threatening sword in the creature's hand as a symbol of God's displeasure with him and the whole nation of Israel.[3] He therefore questioned whether their commitment to God's Torah was wanting. Did God send you to us because we are not fulfilling the Torah "that Moshe commanded *us* (*lanu*)..."[4] No, answered the heavenly man, I have not come to criticize your commitment to the Torah but I *did* come to criticize the people of Israel for their failure to fulfill the intention behind the command,

---

[1] Based on an oral interpretation in the name of the late Ponevezher Rav, Rabbi Yosef Kahaneman *z"l.*

[2] *Yehoshua* 5:13–15.

[3] *Megilla* 7a.

[4] The Gemara understands this statement as a reference to a verse that continues, "...is the heritage of the Congregation of Yakov" (*Devarim* 33:4).

"Now!," as it says in the verse, *"Now,* write this song for yourselves and teach it to the children of Israel."

What does this all mean? Indeed one of the major questions of religious Jewish life is whether one commits himself to Torah because it is an inheritance (i.e., tradition), or because it is truly the song of one's life. Judaism as inheritance functions as a comfortable lifestyle, a heritage that one is happy to continue because of history and values, but not because one's whole life's mission is interwoven with it.

A song however, is something entirely different. Song bubbles up from within a person when he becomes overwhelmed by his experience, or when something touches the deepest levels of his soul. Song expresses meaning beyond the logic of words. An authentic song reveals the ineffable as it protests against the rigidness of a purely verbal mindset.

Such a song never comes about simply from a commitment to a lifestyle. True song bursts forth when a person's whole being becomes absorbed in its deep inner dimensions. Only when one experiences the blur of boundaries between doer and deed, singer and song, can one speak of an authentic religious experience. One must achieve a state of ecstasy in which one no longer sings the song but *is* the song.

This is the reason why the Torah is called a Song. "Now write for yourselves this song," means that a Jew must strive with passion to make his relationship with the Almighty his ongoing raison d'être – his song of life. This verse calls on man to do no less than turn his life into a work of art in which every moment expresses holiness, dignity, and the ultimate beauty.

The renowned poet, Rainer Maria Rilke was once asked by a young admirer whether he should become a poet. He responded, "Only when you cannot live without being a poet." And so it is with a life of Torah. Only when one cannot imagine life without it, does the Torah truly become a song.

10

"Not Yet" Jews By Choice

The story of Yitro, Moshe's father-in-law and a convert to Judaism, poses a challenge that should force us to rethink our Jewishness. Moshe left his wife Tzippora and their children with Yitro when he set out to redeem the Jewish People and lead them miraculously across the Red Sea. After a long period of absence the family reunites in the wilderness.

"Yitro, the father-in-law of Moshe came to Moshe with his sons and wife *to the wilderness* where he was encamped...."[1]

This piece of information – that they met in the wilderness – seems entirely superfluous since everyone knows by this point that Moshe and the children of Israel were wandering in the desert. Rashi, recognizing this seeming redundancy, explains that the inclusion of the extra words here calls attention to the tremendous sacrifice Yitro made when he decided to become a Jew.

"He lived in the world of glory. Still his heart moved him to leave it all behind and to go to the wilderness and hear the words of the Torah."[2]

Indeed Yitro was a man of great wealth. Until he chose to follow Moshe, he was the high priest in Midian,[3] a most prestigious position not unlike that of the Pope's in Rome today. He was surrounded by servants, glory, and extravagance. The verse informs us that he gave up all this material success to go to a barren wasteland, where he would no longer enjoy the pleasures of this world from a position of high honor. As a Jew

---

[1] *Shemot* 18:5.
[2] *ad loc.*
[3] See Rashi on 18:1.

he would become one amongst many, no longer a man of stature in his own right but rather "the father-in-law of Moshe."

In addition, the Torah informs us that Yitro became an outcast in his former home. He had rejected the popular religions and philosophies of his society, and was shunned by his former friends, neighbors, and colleagues. He became a "lonely man of faith" and ended up in the empty desert. Moved by his love for God, Torah, and the Jewish people, Yitro made everything else of secondary importance. His only priority was to be part of the Jewish people and participate in its *mitzvot*.

Yitro confronts us, for the first time after the Exodus, with a new phenomenon – *being a Jew by choice*. And by doing so, he poses a challenge to all future generations of Jews for the rest of history: How to be a Jew by choice when one is born into the Jewish faith? How does one feel the same level of "brenn" – the passionate desire to live as a committed Jew – as Yitro felt? We can only hope to achieve such a goal if we in some way re-enact Yitro's spiritual journey in our own lives. And no doubt he must have traveled a long and difficult road – a heart-rending climb with many setbacks before reaching the top.

To succeed, Yitro must have invented for himself a most important device: A "ladder of observance." Like a baby learning to take its first steps, he must have engaged the world of Halacha slowly, step by step. To feel its touch, to integrate it in his life and to feel absorbed by its spirit, like a man who immerses himself in a swimming pool, one limb at a time, and then swims in the water, touched at all points and conscious everywhere.

We Jews born into the fold must try in our own way, to build our own ladders of observance. To start all over again. To re-engage with *mitzvot* as though we had never heard of them before. Only then can we become "Jews by choice." This does not mean that we should drop all the *mitzvot* that we currently observe and keep only a few. Rather we should begin a process by which we take hold of each mitzvah that we observe already as a matter of course, and transform it into something radically new and uplifting, *as if* we had *never* done it before.

A student once asked the great Jewish philosopher and "ba'al teshuva" Franz Rosenzweig whether or not he put on tefillin.[4] "Not yet" was his answer. Although he may not have felt ready at the time to take on this great mitzvah, he made it clear that he looked forward to the day when forging a connection with God via wearing tefillin would become a reality for him. This does not imply in any way that he was right to delay his performance of this mitzvah. After all, he himself used to say later in his life that "it is in the deed that one hears." Only when one actually takes a leap of faith and *does* a mitzvah can one hear and feel its profundity. We can however, learn from Franz Rozenzweig's statement that by merely putting on tefillin, one has not yet performed the mitzvah to its full extent. Only when one comes to the mitzvah as a novice, like Yitro, not out of tradition or habit, but out of a genuine desire to fulfill the word of God, can one experience the full power of fulfilling the Torah's commandments.

Yitro found this road to Judaism because of his willingness to sacrifice his life of luxury to come close to God. And so, his journey challenges each one of us. How much of Yitro's determination lives within us? To what extent are we Jews by choice? If we had been born into Yitro's world, a world completely removed from anything Jewish, would we have given up fortune and glory to wander into the desert for the privilege to be a Jew? This is Yitro's question, and it requires our honest response.

---

[4] *Teffilin*: phylacteries

47

11

Halacha and "Trivialities"[1]

Judaism is a religion of holy trivialities because Man meets God most intensely in commonplace deeds. God created a world full of seemingly trivial moments in order to show us that every move we make, however small, can have profound significance. To meet God in the synagogue, or in a moment of devotion on Shabbat or Yom Kippur is important, but not the ultimate goal. The goal of religious life is to refine one's lens enough to see God in the mundane, to elevate everyday experiences and transform them into encounters with holiness. This is the art of life – to feel a great passion for God's world while dealing with chores. To hear the beautiful music that hides behind the drone.

This ability is the great gift of Halacha, which imbues every action with eternal significance and allows us to sanctify the physical world. Halacha calls on man to leave the world of the average and reveal God. The intricate details of Jewish Law allow us to rediscover Sinai in every minute aspect of the human experience. Halacha awakens our consciousness and thus allows us to free the holy sparks that would otherwise stay imprisoned within the average.

Because it forces us to sanctify *every* moment and deed, Halacha protects us from making the all-too-common mistake of waiting for sudden moments of epiphany. Nothing is more dangerous to religious life than this kind of passivity – waiting to be swept up in a fleeting moment of great religious fervor, the likes of which come along rarely if

---

[1] The following observations were inspired by the writings of Abraham Joshua Heschel.

at all, without our active input. Without the routine wake-up calls of Halacha, our souls would lie dormant, atrophying for lack of "exercise."

There is an important spiritual lesson in this: We must not only sanctify the goal, but also the path to the goal. We may not be able to reach our destination immediately, but we can ensure that we are on the right road.

Scientists dedicate their lives to the most minute properties of the physical world. They are fascinated with the behaviors of cells, the habits of insect species, and the peculiarities of the DNA code. It is often not so much the broad picture that fascinates them, but rather singular details that serve as the subjects of their investigations. So too, great Halachic authorities tremble over the smallest aspects of human life. They peer deep within every human act, utterance, thought, and intention, in search of the moral dimension – to discover the divine in every detail. Nothing is deemed too insignificant to warrant their attention.

Just as many anti-intellectual cynics consider scientists to be guilty of self-torture and indulgence for sitting for months behind a microscope watching tiny cell movements, so too the irreligious often cannot understand why the religious man worries about which blessing is the most appropriate to make over his bowl of soup. But for the scientist and the observant Jew unraveling the mystery that hides within a small detail, discovering its source and implications, and thus learning how to respond to it, turns an encounter with the commonplace (like cells and soup) into one of the great privileges and pleasures available to mankind. Only when he frequently encounters the infinite in this way can a man claim that he really lives.

12

The Waters of Strife:
Religious Coercion or Gentle Persuasion?

For centuries, commentators have struggled with, and argued about, the incident of the *"Mei-Meriva"* – the waters of strife. After the children of Israel complained about the lack of water in the desert, God ordered Moshe to *speak* to a rock and draw forth water, but, as is well known, he *hit* the rock instead.[1]

Moshe was punished harshly for his failure to adhere strictly to the details of this command. Indeed, his ultimate dream to enter and live in the land of Israel was shattered because of this one seemingly small mistake, and in spite of all his pleas for forgiveness, God did not allow him to lead the Israelites across the Jordan. God's severity in this narrative is unprecedented. Four times the Torah refers to this divine expression of "anger," and five times God condemns Moshe for this sin: 1. "Because *you* did not believe in Me." 2. "*You* rebelled against Me." 3. "*You* rebelled against My commandment." 4. "*You* trespassed against Me." 5. "*You* did not sanctify Me in the midst of the Children of Israel."[2]

The sin is even more perplexing since causing water to gush forth from a rock by hitting it, is no less miraculous than producing the same effect via speech. Only one slight blow produced enough water to quench millions of people's thirst. No scientific explanation could ever account for this! What in Moshe's actions entailed such flagrant disbelief and rebellion so as to warrant such a harsh response? What changed as a result of Moshe's decision to hit the rock rather than speak to it? What was lost? And why did God insist that water be produced miraculously by

---

[1] *Bamidbar*, chapter 20.
[2] *Bamidbar* 20:12–13, 20:23–24; *Devarim* 27:12–14, 32:48–51.

speech and nothing else? Why did He not leave this seemingly small matter in Moshe's domain? After all, *Torah lo bashamayim hi!*

Paraphrasing Sophocles in his *Philoctetes*, we could say, "I see that everywhere among the race of men, it is the tongue that wins and not the coercive act." Hitting implies coercion – a brute force that does not leave the Other with any alternative option other than to do whatever they are told by their attacker. To refuse in the face of physical force is nearly impossible. Hence, obedience does not demonstrate any real willingness or agreement with the actions that follow as a result. Even the threat of physical coercion casts suspicion on one's deeds, and thus obscures its *authenticity* – and usually implies a complete lack of authenticity.

Speech on the other hand, is a means of persuasion that does not bypass or disable the agent's decision-making processes. Any response to speech will therefore be genuine and authentic.[3]

In many ways the revelation at Sinai was an intensely coercive event. This position is borne out in the famous remark by the Talmud that God threatened to drop the mountain on top of the Israelites if they chose not to accept the Torah.[4] Rabbi Aha ben Yakov protests this assertion – that if God indeed threatened to kill the Jews if they refused to be party to the covenant, then this calls into question the legality of the agreement, which implies that perhaps the Jewish people are not really obligated to keep the commandments in the Torah! Some Chassidic masters suggest that it was this threat, this feeling of having been forced, that led to the sin of the golden calf![5] If so, it would seem that the overkill was a bit too much for the Israelites to bear and thus became counter-productive at a certain level.

That said, the world was only created so that the Jewish people would accept the Torah. Sometimes coercion can be for a person's benefit and often serves as an essential ingredient of his education.

---

[3] This is alluded to by *Meshech Chochma*, ad loc. See also *Maharal*.
[4] *Shabbat* 88a.
[5] See for example: *Chidushei HaRim, Parashat Yitro.*

Homines enim civiles non nascuntur, sed fiunt,[6] said Spinoza, reflecting an old Jewish truth. But Law must ultimately lead to moral freedom. This means that liberty is above all a problem of education. To be an agent of freedom and not constraint, lawful coercion must lead to an awareness in man that had he understood them, he would have accepted the values inherent in the law by even the most gentle forms of persuasion.

King David expressed this concept when he said: "I will walk in freedom, for I have sought out Your law."[7] By a beautiful exegetical pun, the Sages read the description of the tablets on which God wrote the Ten Commandments not as "the writing of God "engraved" *(charut)* on the tablets, but as "freedom" *(cherut)* on the tablets."[8] Only when we engrave the law into our hearts, do we experience absolute freedom – that is, self-expression in the deepest and truest sense of the term.[9]

When standing at the border of the land of Israel, the Jewish people underwent a radical change of "weltanschauung." At Sinai, and during their years of wandering in the desert, God used coercion as a necessary device to ready them for lives as Jews. Suddenly, as they entered the land and became more spiritually independent, they came to understand that the survival of Judaism would rest on the effectiveness of gentle persuasion. While bound by the Law, they realized that to build a deeply religious society, Jewish educators would need to use the power of the word – gentle and inspiring – and not the rod, if they hoped to foster

---

[6] *"For civil men are not born but made"* – Benedictus Spinoza, See T.H Green, *Principles of Political Obligation*, p. 53, Longman, Green &Co, Ltd., London.
[7] *Tehillim* 119:45.
[8] *Pirkei Avot* 6:2.
[9] Note: This is not what the British philosopher Isaiah Berlin calls "negative liberty" (i.e., freedom *from...*), but rather a constitutional freedom in which one's freedom automatically respects the freedom of the other and for which one is prepared to make sacrifices. Otherwise, "Freedom for the pike means death to the minnows..." See: "Two Concepts of Liberty" in *Four Essays on Liberty*, pp. 118–173 where Berlin explains this at great length.

conditions in which Jews would be *willing* and feel *privileged* to live their lives according to the Torah's mandate.

Had this not become clear at the inception of the first Jewish Commonwealth, the nation's government could have become a tyrannical and fundamentalist dictatorship. This mode of leadership would have been a sign of weakness (do the Jews have to be beaten into observing God's law?) calling into question the inherent truth and persuasive powers of the Torah. What could profane God's name more than this? So we see that this was the problem at the core of Moshe's sin. For the sake of later generations who would need to know that the way of the Torah is found in the gentle word, and not in the hard strike, God denied Moshe the merit of living in the land. Thus, He made it clear to all, that leaders who seek to turn Israel into a holy nation by threat or by force may bring disaster to themselves and to their people.

13

Halachic Toleration of Heresy:
A Command to Cancel the Commandments[1]

Halacha deals with human life on intellectual and emotional levels. As such Halachic requirements function against a backdrop of dialectical tension. Sometimes the law must favor cold calculation, and at other times it must give more weight to providing necessary guidance for men with a propensity for irrationality and inevitable emotional upheavals. Most of the time, Halacha acts effectively to channel man's emotional states into a meaningful purpose in order to bring him back to the path of reason and religious thinking.

In one case, however, Halacha allows man's emotions to have the upper hand without imposing restraints or boundaries.

"One whose dead relative lies in front of him is exempt from the recital of the *Shema* and from prayer and from *Teffilin* and from all [positive] precepts laid down in the Torah."[2]

This is a most remarkable and revolutionary ruling which runs contrary to conventional Halachic thinking. Why should a person whose dead relative is not yet buried become free from the Torah's (positive) requirements for a day? Did God not give us the *mitzvot* so that we would observe them at *all* times? Since when is one able to cancel the commandments?

This ruling becomes even more puzzling when one considers that fulfilling *mitzvot* at such a time of tremendous upheaval and confusion

---

[1] The following observations were inspired by Rabbi Yosef Ber Soloveitchik's Eulogy for the Talner Rebbe, Rabbi M.Z. Twersky *z"l, Shiure Rav,* edited by Yosef Epstein. Ktav, NJ, 1974.

[2] *Berachot* 17b.

would provide a mourner with religious meaning and could therefore be of great therapeutic value. Is man not *most* in need of religious support at this bitter moment? Would it not be the proper role of Judaism to step in and offer man consolation and order through ritual requirements that would bring him into close contact with God? In this way he might be able to deal with his loss. Why relieve man of his religious obligations just when he most needs them?

After deeper reflection on this problem, one cannot but marvel at Halacha's profound grasp of human psychology. Recognizing the full emotional impact of losing a close relative, the Halacha allows for a most unusual state: *Momentary heresy.*

Before burial, while the dead remains (literally) "still in front of us" it is almost impossible for a man to stay fully religious. At this hour, the doubts set in – regarding God's justice and even regarding His very existence. How could a loving God do this to me? Why did my loved one have to die? Man's fright and confusion at this moment is too overwhelming for rational arguments, which he may know well, to demonstrate God's existence, unceasing kindness, and unfathomable wisdom. As such the Halacha tolerates the mourner's torturous and somewhat heretical thoughts, and does not try to repress them. Because of the Law's great compassion for the suffering human being, "it permitted the mourner to have his way for a while and has ruled that the latter is relieved from all *mitzvot.*"[3] How can one ask a mourner to say *brachot* or tefillot when it is impossible for him to back up his words with appropriate kavana?

Only after burial, when the dead is no longer in front of the mourner, can the spiritual healing process begin. From that moment onwards Halacha once again obligates the mourner to observe all precepts. His doubts still linger, but at this stage the Halacha activates the

---

[3] *Shiure Rav*, page 67. Also see Tosafot's (*Berachot* 17b: *Patur MeKriyat Shema*) remarkable observation that one can only observe the commandments when one is busy with life, not with death!

concept of "Na'aseh V'nishma" – "We shall do and [then] we will be able to hear," as the Israelites exclaimed at Sinai.

Judaism's recognition of God is not the triumphant outcome of philosophical investigation but from the enlightenment that comes through performance of *mitzvot*. Through the observance of the commandments we perceive and internalize the wisdom of the Commander. In *doing*, one *perceives*. In carrying out the word of the Torah, man reconnects himself to the everlasting covenant and regains his certainty of God's presence. The Divine, after all, sings in the *mitzvot*.

After burial, once the shock of death loses some of its initial impact, Halacha reminds man that he is by definition a "homo religiosus" and that as such, there is no escape from God and His will.[4] No doubt, the healing process takes a long time, but it can only begin when one returns to his life and remembers that he lives in the presence of God.[5]

---

[4] The conventional reason for the dispensation of precepts at this hour is the Halachic ruling *"Osek baMitzvot patur memitzvot,"* when one is fully occupied with a mitzvah, in our case the preparations for the burial, one is free (discharged from the obligation) from all other *mitzvot*. This however does not explain why other relatives who are not fully occupied with the burial are also forbidden to pray etc. Still, according to most authorities the same rule applies. Our interpretation, however, fully explains why this is so.

[5] It should be noted that the mourner is only free and forbidden to observe the *positive* precepts. The *prohibitions* (forbidding commandments) continue to apply since the dispensation of them would create havoc in the person and destroy the fabric of the Jewish society. One may also argue that the observance of the prohibitions are not so much to build the need to recognize God but to prevent negative conditions which makes the recognition much harder. Obviously the mourner who is already shaken in his beliefs should not be helped to deepen his possible disbelief.

14

Mixing With This World and Washing Your Hands of It

In an unusual passage, the Talmud reports that King Solomon instituted the laws concerning the Eruv (i.e., "mixing of the realms") through which one is allowed to carry objects from one domain to another on Shabbat, which would otherwise be forbidden.[1] The Talmud goes on to say that on another occasion King Solomon instituted the ritual washing of the hands. Both decrees were received with Divine favor and a heavenly voice issued forth and proclaimed, "My son, if your heart is wise, Mine will be glad…"[2]

The great Chassidic Sage, Rabbi Menachem Mendel of Kotzk, wondered what great wisdom lies hidden within these laws, such that the Heavenly Master was moved to joyfully approve of them in such a public manner. In his typically profound way, the Kotzker Rebbe explained that both laws demonstrate that a Jew must be both involved ("mixed") in the world and simultaneously separated enough "to wash one's hands of it."

This observation is all the more remarkable since King Solomon was known for being deeply involved in the world (e.g., he negotiated international trade agreements and peace treaties, organized public works projects, adjudicated legal cases, etc.) and tasted all of its pleasures. Nevertheless, he maintained, according to the Kotzker Rebbe, a certain distance from the world so that he could detach from it when necessary.

To eat, to drink, to be fully involved, and yet to remain somehow disconnected from the world is indeed a great challenge, and to accomplish this feat requires great wisdom.

---

[1] *Eruvin* 21b.
[2] See *Mishlei* 23:15.

When looking into the construction of the Mishkan, the Tabernacle, built in the days of Moshe, we find another expression of the same idea. As is well known, the Israelites constructed the Tabernacle in the desert, and afterwards brought it into the land of Israel to become the center of their Divine worship. Once they entered the land, the Jews ceased to live in a world of constant, open miracles, but suddenly found themselves obligated to build for themselves a society that would be both political and deeply religious.

This too, was quite a challenge. A successful spiritual culture requires more than just the bare essentials. To foster religious fervor, the Jewish people needed some beauty and refinement (e.g., art and music), which are to some degree, necessary to nourish the religious being. Taken too far, though, luxuries can easily become an impediment to holiness, particularly when they are seen as goals in themselves. As such, a society needs them, but must simultaneously work to keep them connected to the Infinite.

When carefully observing the human condition, we can divide our needs into three categories:

1. *Essential* – for example, food, clothing, and shelter which are the elementary requirements for human existence.

2. *Useful* – anything that makes life easier, but without which we could still survive (e.g., roads, bridges, tools, and other forms of technology).

3. *Ornamental* – arts that have no practical value but which elevate the quality of our lives, and make the human experience more pleasant.

At all three levels, fulfilling these needs can be part of religious enrichment. However, taken past the point of moderation, each has the potential for great social evils – over-indulgence, envy, class struggle, corruption, etc.

When looking into the plans for the Tabernacle's construction, we see that *all* three categories were represented. Some items were absolutely essential to the Tabernacle, such as the outer shell (shelter).

Other elements (e.g., the ramp leading up to the altar) functioned solely to make the priests' jobs easier. Certain fineries were also added that had no apparent practical value whatsoever, but greatly enhanced the beauty of the Tabernacle and the religious experience of those who worshipped there (e.g., the ornate embroidery and vivid dyes).

Jewish tradition states that every category of creative work was represented in the Tabernacle. As such, any human activity that was not needed at any phase in building the Mishkan does not have the status of "work" *(melacha)* in Judaism.

When we put all these pieces together, a very clear message starts to emerge. Before the Jews began building their political state, they first built a place of worship that required them to employ every manner of craftsmanship and labor that they would ever use in the construction of their nation. To make sure that they aligned their priorities correctly, and fully integrated the idea that nothing should ever become an object of over-indulgence, the Jewish people gave their initial bursts of creativity and labor to God. And so they dedicated their thoughts and talents – which would soon be used in the establishment of their new homeland – to Divine service.

As the people toiled to make the Tabernacle and all its accessories, the vestments and various articles, they remained constantly aware of God and their mission as members of a holy nation. Later, when they used these same skills in their mundane day-to-day lives, they recalled that the very first time they involved themselves in such work, it was for purely spiritual-religious purposes. As such they were able to maintain an elevated state of consciousness while involved in their daily occupations.[3]

---

[3] This highly original observation is mentioned by Rabbi Yisachar Yakovson in *Iyunim BeParashiyoth HaTorah*, Sinai Publishing House, Tel Aviv, 1977, *Parashat Tetzaveh*, in the name of Moses Mendelsohn. Obviously many other symbolic, ethical and philosophical reasons have been given for the tabernacle and all its items.

Via this ingenious training program, the Jewish people were able to mix with worldly affairs and at the same time, knew how to artfully "wash their hands of it." This ability to stay mentally focused on spiritual matters, while physically engaging with the world, is the wisdom the Kotzker Rebbe recognized in King Solomon's dual decrees – the mixing of the realms and the washing of the hands.

15

Frontal Encounter and Faith

Faith is deeper than knowledge. While scientific investigation expands the mind, the products of faith refine and edify the totality of a human being. Close contact with spirituality touches us at all levels and leaves us, everywhere, transformed. Because its effects are so much more radical, it is much more difficult to achieve faith than to acquire knowledge.

Faith is an awe-inspiring challenge, especially in times of hardship and depression. One must expend huge efforts to cherish it, maintain it, and make it grow.

King David's verse, "To declare Your steadfast love in the morning and Your faithfulness by night"[1] describes beautifully the trial of authentic faith. The deeper meaning seems to be as follows: If one feels the brightness of the morning, makes that the basis of his faith, and consequently sings God's praise, then in the loneliness of the night when evidence of this Divine attribute can no longer be found, only the truly faithful will manage to continue to believe in God's greatness.

Moshe prayed: "Show me now Your glory." He was eager to understand God's presence and His ways of dealing with the world and with every human being. God responded: "You shall see My back, but My face shall not be seen."[2]

Within this cryptic interaction lies great meaning. Much of what we see in this world looks topsy-turvy, confused and contrary to what human reason expects to find. The world stands with its back to reason. It is not that Moshe saw God's back. Rather he saw the front from the perspective of the back. It was as if he got to look at an X-ray taken from

---

[1] *Tehillim* 92:3.
[2] *Shemot* 33:23.

hindsight whereby what is last is really the first and what is in front is really in the back.

Had God shown Moshe the front as the front and the back as the back, everything would have made sense. Possessing this knowledge – this blazing clarity of thought – would have killed him, literally. No human, by nature bound by time, could ever experience this intense confrontation and survive.

To die is to be permitted to see the full story, unshielded, without the need to see the front by way of the back. For some it takes a lifetime to realize this; for others it is altogether beyond their grasp. But some individuals, however young, seize it at a moment's notice, and are therefore asked to come home.

16

The Blessings of Ephraim and Menashe

"Man always dies before he is fully born."
–Erich Fromm

A person can only know with certainty that he succeeded in educating his children when he sees the conduct of his grandchildren. And even then one cannot be entirely sure.

The Torah, in a most undeviating way, alerts us to the extreme difficulty of successful parenting in the story of Yakov Avinu's struggles with his children's upbringing. In particular, the way he handled his sons' delicate relationships is a source of considerable controversy.[1] After demonstrating a greater level of love and devotion to his son Yosef, the brothers became embroiled in a major rift which ultimately led to one of the great tragedies in Jewish history – the enslavement of the people of Israel in Egypt for 210 years.

One would readily be able to forgive Yakov for making this mistake if the root of the problem lay in his relative inexperience in the field of education. But if that were the case, why then did he make the same mistake when dealing with his grandchildren? Why did he openly favor Yosef's children over the children of his other sons? Indeed, Yakov only seems interested in Yosef's sons Ephraim and Menashe. After all, we never read a single word about the other brothers' sons, nor do we hear anything about Yakov's relationships with them. This complete silence is telling. Yakov only seems to have given time and attention to Ephraim and Menashe. Only with *them* did he converse. Even more astonishing is

---

[1] *Bereishit* 37.

the fact that they were the only grandchildren who received Yakov's special blessings before he died.

As if this were not enough blatant favoritism, Yakov openly favored one of Yosef's sons over the other! When blessing Ephraim and Menashe, Yakov went out of his way to bless the younger (Ephraim) before the older (Menashe)![2] Did he not remember the disastrous consequences of showing this sort of bias in front of his own sons? Should he not have learned his lesson by now? No longer can we excuse Yakov's behavior with the claim of youthful inexperience and indiscretion!

Rabbi Yakov Kamenetsky, in his monumental work *Emeth LeYakov*, calls our attention to the difference between the names that Yosef gave his two sons. Both, as is well known, were born in Egypt. When the oldest was born, Yosef called him Menashe, *ki nashini Elokim*. Rabbi Samson Rafael Hirsch translates this verse as, "because God has made my trouble and all my paternal house into creditors to me." When his second son was born, Yosef named him Ephraim, "because God has made me blossom (*ki hifrani Elokim*) in the land of my affliction."[3] There is a most remarkable difference between these two names.

When naming Menashe, Yosef made reference to the pain of living in a foreign country with strong feelings of nostalgia for his father's house. Although he thrived in, and even ruled, his foreign home, his whole personality objected and rebelled against Egypt's idolatrous culture. He refused to take part in it, however deeply involved he became in its governmental administration. By the time Yosef had to choose a name for his second son Ephraim, however, it seems that some kind of metamorphosis had taken place within him. While he was still aware of his unusual position as an Israelite in a strange land, he had somehow

---

[2] *Bereishit* 48.
[3] *Bereishit* 41:51, 52.

come to feel more comfortable in his new home. "God has made me blossom in the land of my affliction."[4]

The distinction is most telling. While there is little doubt that Yosef remained, throughout all his life, first and foremost an Israelite, the anti-Israelite climate in Egypt obviously exerted an influence. Yosef had to adapt himself, at least externally, to survive and succeed in his new environment, and this must have played a role in shaping his ultimate identity. Often, a person remains unaware of very slight changes taking place within his personality. Assimilation is a slow and, at the start, unrecognizable process. It is only when others make us aware, that we start to realize what we have become.

From this perspective Yakov's choices as a grandfather become more comprehensible. Ephraim and Menashe were the only two grandchildren who were not born and raised in close proximity to Yakov. While the other grandchildren grew up in Yakov's home, nurtured by the land of Israel, Ephraim and Menashe came of age in a foreign country and never got to experience their grandfather and the nurturing environment of his thoroughly "Jewish" home.

Surely this must have worried Yakov greatly. The question of how these grandchildren would maintain their "Jewish" identities in such spiritually hostile surroundings must have been on his mind constantly. Yakov therefore proclaims to Yosef, "Now your sons who were born to you in the land of Egypt before I came to you in Egypt, are mine; Ephraim and Menashe shall be mine like Reuven and Shimon."[5] In other words, I will have to draw them back into the family before they are lost.

This interpretation, however, does not explain why he favored Ephraim over Menashe.

By looking beneath the surface, we can conclude that there must have been a major difference in the education these two sons received. By

---

[4] This can also be seen from the fact that Ephraim is not so much a Jewish as an Egyptian name. It is similar to the words, Pharao, Potifar, and Shifra.
[5] *Bereishit* 48.

the time Ephraim was born, Yosef, not yet fully involved with the administration of Egypt and still more of a foreigner, had already made an indelible mark on his son Menashe's young psyche. Surely Yosef communicated clearly that, *Although I am the second ruler in this country, always remember that this does not effect my loyalty towards my God and my people. We are first and foremost Israelites.*

But by the time Ephraim was born, Yosef's feelings of being a foreigner had faded somewhat; and without the constant reinforcement of a strong and unwavering message of Jewish identification, his younger son's development was necessarily more vulnerable to external influences.[6]

As such, Yakov was right to worry more about Ephraim's spiritual training than Menashe's. He knew that Ephraim was much more susceptible to the "kulturgesellschaft" of Egypt, having grown up in the sweet but toxic atmosphere of Pharaoh's palace. It was therefore necessary, for the sake of the future of the Jewish people, for Yakov to give more time to Ephraim than to Menashe. He needed to instill in him "Jewish" values and to uproot the negative influences from his childhood. Menashe, by contrast, came from a relatively stronger "Jewish" background and hence needed less special attention. Clearly this was even more the case for the rest of his grandchildren, all of whom were born in the land of Israel and raised at Yakov's knees. No doubt all of them were well-aware of their assimilated cousin's precarious situation, and may have even have encouraged Yakov to give Ephraim more of his time and attention.

This could also explain why Yakov placed his right hand on Ephraim's head, and gave him a stronger blessing than his older brother. Since he was more exposed to the culture of Egypt, he and his descendents would need a greater level of encouragement and Divine assistance. In taking this approach, we see that Yakov in fact, did not

---

[6] According to this interpretation, some extended time must have passed between the births of the two brothers, which is unclear in the text.

repeat the mistake of favoring one child over another without specific cause and proper reason.

Most interesting is the fact that the child who suffered more from exposure to external influences was destined to overtake his brother, who received a much better "Jewish" education. Yakov explicitly states about Menashe that, "He will also become a people, and he also will be great, nevertheless, his younger brother will be greater than he, and his seed shall become full to the nations."[7] This is indeed a remarkable turn around. Why should the child who was more exposed to the secular world have a brighter future than the one who received a much stronger and more traditional education? We have already alluded to this issue with regards to Moshe Rabeinu, who was raised by a non-Jewish mother and educated in Pharaoh's palace, and nevertheless grew up to become the greatest Jewish prophet, leader, and man in history.[8] Were there no better candidates? Perhaps someone blessed with a proper Jewish educational background? Why select an assimilated Jewish boy who may not have even known that he was an Israelite until later in life?

We explained that perhaps a person who has to fight for his Jewish identity will, in the end, have more courage and strength to stand up to outside influences precisely because he has participated in, and gained a familiarity with, the outside world. Moshe was the ideal leader *because* he was raised in a culture that opposed Jewish values and thus had to prove and build his character through many inner spiritual battles.

Looking into the blessing that Yakov gave to Ephraim, we encounter a similar idea. Yakov tells him that he will "become full to the nations." While there exist many possible explanations for this unusual expression, we may suggest that Ephraim's tribe would, more than any other, possess the power to stand strong against the forces of assimilation. Rashi clearly alludes to this in his commentary when he

---

[7] *Bereishit* 48:19.

[8] See *Thoughts To Ponder: Daring Observations About The Jewish Tradition*, Nathan Lopes Cardozo Urim Publications, New York, Jerusalem, 2002.

writes, "All the world will be filled with the glory [of Yehoshua who was a descendant of Ephraim] when his fame and his name will go forth...."

It is most revealing that Jewish parents have blessed their children since ancient times with the blessing suggested by Yakov Avinu: "With you shall Israel bless, saying: May God make you as Ephraim and Menashe."

Yakov expressed herewith the delicate balance between the need for a strong "Jewish" identity and the capacity to interact with the outside world. Finding this middle path is far from easy, and trying to do so has been a source of constant problems throughout Jewish history. Too much introversion leads to dangerous isolation, because it soon becomes impossible to relate to the greater community of human beings, which in turn prevents us from fulfilling our function as a "light unto the nations." Too much adaptation, however, brings with it an essential loss of identity which leads inevitably to assimilation and devastation. To locate the right equilibrium requires a special blessing, indeed, and this is precisely what we hope for our children when we bless them with the words of Yakov Avinu, grandfather par excellence.

17

Religious Hypocrisy

"With devotion's visage
And pious action
We do sugar o'er
The devil himself."
–Shakespeare, *Hamlet*, 3.1.47

Kosher animals, as is well known, can be identified by two *simanim* (physical signs). They have to chew their cud, *and* their hooves must be wholly cloven.[1] In order to be kosher, the animal must possess both *simanim*. The Torah goes out of its way to emphasize the fact that an animal in which only one sign is present, cannot be considered kosher in any way.

"The camel, because it chews its cud but does not part the hoof, it is unclean unto you. And the rock-badger, because it chews its cud but does not part the hoof, it is unclean to you. And the hare, because it chews its cud but does not part the hoof, it is unclean to you. And the swine, because it parts the hoof and is cloven-footed, but does not chew the cud, it is unclean to you."[2]

Carefully reading this text makes us wonder. Why did the Torah need to state that these non-kosher animals chew their cuds or have cloven hooves? After all, that is *not* what makes them unclean. On the contrary having one positive sign suggests that perhaps they could be kosher! If the Torah had only mentioned the negative indicators in these animals that clearly identify them as non-kosher, we would have

---

[1] *Vayikra*, chapter 11, and *Devarim*, chapter 14.
[2] *Vayikra*, 11:4–8.

concluded that they are indeed not clean, since we know that the Torah requires an animal to possess two signs, and not just one, to be kosher.

On top of this, why are first the kosher signs of these non-kosher animals mentioned and only afterwards the non-kosher signs? The Torah should have written them in the reverse order! Surely their non-kosher signs bear more relevance in a discussion of why these animals are not kosher!

Rabbi Ephraim Shlomo ben Chaim of Luntshitz, known as the Keli Yakar (1550–1619) gives us a most illuminating explanation for why the Torah specifically chose this wording and no other. In his opinion, we might have thought that indeed, the non-kosher aspects of these animals make them impure, but that the kosher signs somehow ameliorate that impurity. Therefore the Torah came to tell us that *the* kosher signs of non-kosher animals make them all the more unclean.

This carries with it a most important message. Animals with only one kosher sign represent a most serious, negative character trait – hypocrisy. The camel or the swine give the *appearance* of being kosher. The camel can demonstrate its *kashrut* by emphasizing that it does, after all, chew its cud. The swine, too, can hold out its cloven hooves in order to "prove" its virtue. Both therefore have the ability to hide their true natures behind a facade of purity. Only upon close inspection, do we realize that these animals are unclean.

They are waving a kosher flag, but hiding unclean cargo.

This is indeed much worse than being completely non-kosher. Completely non-kosher animals, at least, do not try to deceive us about their impurity, but rather openly and honestly declare "where they stand." With the other animals, there is no hypocrisy – no misleading impressions. For this reason, the Torah mentions the kosher signs of the camel and the swine first, for these misleading signs make them even more unclean!

When reading the story about Yakov's gift of the colored garment to Yosef, the Torah states, "And they [the brothers] saw that

Yakov loved Yosef more than his brothers, they hated him and they could not speak peaceably with him."[3] On this verse, Rashi comments, "From their blame we learn their praise, for they did not speak one way with their mouths and another way in their hearts." Even in their error, we see that they were honest, and this is praiseworthy.

This message cannot be emphasized enough in our troubled times. The damage done by those who represent religious doctrines, quasi-Judaisms, or other religions, who speak a double language, is unforgivable. Hiding one's dishonesty behind religious texts, talmudic knowledge, religious garments, and frequent visits to houses of prayer, desecrates the name of God, and disparages genuine religion.

"Let them not forget that hypocrites may deceive the cleverest and most penetrating man, but the least wide-awake of children recognizes it and is revolted by it, however ingeniously it may be disguised."[4]

---

[3] *Bereishit* 37:4.
[4] Leo Tolstoy, *Anna Karenina*, 3:9.

18

Educating Kohanim and the Privilege of Difference

"And the Lord spoke to Moshe – Tell the Kohanim (priests), the children of Aaron, and say to them, 'For a corpse among his people, he shall not defile himself.'"[1] With these words the Torah introduces a complex set of laws that apply only to the family of Aaron, whose special honor it is to serve in the Temple as priests. But perhaps the most notable of these dictums – which still has ramifications for Kohanim even today – is the first, which prohibits the Kohanim from becoming contaminated (with some exceptions) by the spiritual impurity associated with dead bodies. Practically this means that they may not touch a corpse, even to be involved with its burial.

Most remarkable is the fact that the Torah introduces this prohibition with an excess of formality and prefacing: "Speak to the priests, the children of Aaron...*and say to them*..." Why the redundancy? Would it not have been sufficient to say: "Tell the children of Aaron, 'For a corpse among his people, he shall not defile himself'"?

Rashi, in his commentary, directs us to a statement in the Talmud that justifies the extra words in this expression, which apparently refer to the relationship between fathers and their children and the need "to warn the elders concerning the youth." [2] This means that the older Kohanim have an obligation to make sure the younger ones (i.e., those who are not yet 13 years and one day old and therefore not yet bar mitzvah and fully responsible for their actions) do not defile themselves either.

The problem with this explanation, though, is that it does not seem to fully clarify the need for the Torah's twofold expression. First of

---

[1] *Vayikra*, 21:1.
[2] *Yevamot* 114a.

all, Jewish Law always obligates parents to teach their children not to transgress any and every prohibition, even when their children have not yet reached the age of bar mitzvah (or in the case of girls, bat mitzvah – at 12 years and one day). This is a requisite part of every child's Jewish education. Certainly parents have a responsibility to acclimate their children to observing the laws of the Torah so that by the time they reach maturity they will be fully committed and able to live life as Jews.

This being the case, why did the Torah need an extra reminder for Kohanim to train their children to obey the laws that apply only to them?

A second question arises when we look at the two other cases in which the sages make use of the expression, "to warn the elders concerning the youth." In neither instance – the prohibition against eating insects,[3] and the prohibition against consuming blood[4] – is there a seemingly redundant repetition ("tell them" and "say to them") as in our case.

Rabbi Zalman Sorotzkin (1881–1966) ז״ל, the famous Rabbi of Lutzk, offered a most remarkable answer to our question. In the case of the prohibition against eating insects and blood, the warning seems to imply that parents must make sure that they do not cause their children to ingest insects or blood, even when the children would have no knowledge of what they were eating.[5]

But in the case of the Kohanim we are confronted with a completely different kind of educational problem. After all, a child is not only educated by his parents and teachers. He or she is also greatly influenced by the so-called "street," which often promotes values and lifestyles that are far removed from the ones parents try their best to teach in the home. Even when parents and teachers expend great efforts

---

[3] *Vayikra* 11:42.
[4] Ibid 17:12.
[5] This is my understanding of the words of Rabbi Sorotzkin; alternative explanations are possible.

to educate a child, the overwhelming power of the "street" is, in many cases, capable of undoing it all. Children are after all, most impressionable. Parents should consider themselves greatly blessed when they are able to raise their children in an environment that instills the same positive messages that the child receives at home. This is the reason why religious Jews throughout the ages have done everything in their power to make sure their children are educated in Jewish schools within primarily Jewish neighborhoods – so that when the parents tell their children to eat kosher, to observe Sabbath, and not to speak evil about their fellow men, their instructions are reinforced and supported by the general environment. To educate a Jewish child in an alien culture that fundamentally opposes Jewish values, is a phenomenally difficult task.

We can understand then, that Kohanim are faced with a unique parenting challenge. Even when they live in a completely *Jewish* environment, they still face a major problem in educating their children as *Kohanim*. There is, after all, no support-system. Most of the other religious children and neighbors are not Kohanim. They are "just" Israelites and do not have, for example, any obligation to stay away from the dead. In fact they are *obligated* to attend to the dead, and to bury them as fast as possible! As such the Kohen-parent cannot rely on a support system offered by even the most observant, well-meaning, and nurturing "street." For a Kohen, all streets are alien.

Consequently, the parents of young Kohanim have an especially difficult task in making sure that their children will observe all the laws that relate only to them. Perhaps this is the reason why the Torah repeats itself here. The apparent excess in the statements, "tell the Kohanim, the children of Aaron" and "say to them," teaches the parents of Kohanim that they will need to *constantly* emphasize and repeat to their children that they are Kohanim, that they have to follow a special set of rules, and that they are not, for example, allowed to defile themselves by coming into contact with the dead or burial (except for one's very closest blood relatives).

This observation has profound ramifications for Jewish education in general. On one hand, every Jewish child should be surrounded by a system that will promote Jewish values and learning. Nothing is more crucial for the child's education. Especially during its younger years, the child must be brought up in a fully committed and uncompromising Jewish environment. At the same time, nowhere does the Torah suggest that the Kohanim should live in separate enclaves to ensure that no confusing influences from the non-Kohanim will affect the young priests.[6]

Rather, parents and teachers are expected to make an extra effort to educate a child in a way that makes being a Kohen a source of pride. The child should be made to feel special for being *different* and not in any way handicapped because he is a Kohen. After all, the child-Kohen *will* eventually encounter the outside world. Proper and profound Jewish education should be able to inspire the child to live up to his (or her) responsibilities as a member of the priesthood even when they are surrounded by other Jews and even non-Jews, who don't have to abide by such high standards of purity.

The child-Kohen is therefore the product of two opposing philosophies. He needs to live in a full Jewish environment. On the other hand he needs to be able to stand on his own and greatly treasure his uniqueness. In other words, the Torah can only grant the child a *certain* level of protection, but is not willing to put priests in quarantine as a means to prevent any and all deleterious influences. *It is, after all, the distinction that comes from being surrounded by different people, that develops the child's Kohen-related feelings of pride and self-respect.*

The same is true for every Jewish child. Children obviously need a strong, nurturing environment, conducive to their development as committed Jews. However, Jewish education should instill the child with

---

[6] In biblical times the *Kohanim* used to live together with the Levites in special towns. Levites have, however, no obligation to stay away from the dead or observe other laws related to the status of a Kohen.

so much pride that, in later life, he or she will be able to deal with the outside world without feeling in any way insecure or inferior. Jewish children should know how to interact with other cultures, without needing or wanting to join them.

Achieving this goal is the great mission of parents and teachers; it is indeed, a most awesome responsibility.

19

The Successful Failure

Many of the greatest people in history failed time and again before they finally made it to the top. Others thought of themselves as failures, and only realized at a later stage in life that what they believed were defeats were in fact grand successes. Still others never succeeded in the conventional sense of the word, but nevertheless became renowned for their marvelous accomplishments – sometimes without ever being aware of it.

When we carefully study the life of Moshe Rabeinu, we see, quite surprisingly, a long series of failures. Until his eighties he spent most of his time on the run, avoiding danger without getting anywhere or achieving anything. After a short period of childhood tranquility at the palace of Pharaoh, Moshe killed an Egyptian and had to flee the country to avoid prosecution and an inevitable death sentence. He spent many years in different countries, often hiding from the soldiers of the Egyptian regime, never enjoying a quiet moment.

There is little doubt that when he reached the age of eighty, just before God called to him, he must have thought that his life, and all his spectacular potential, had gone to waste. His people were enslaved, and he was a fugitive, an ex-con – just a lowly shepherd trying to earn his daily bread, running around in circles.

After God called to him at the burning bush and he consequently went to liberate his people from bondage, he was met yet again by crushing defeat. His first encounter with Pharaoh was a complete failure. Instead of getting the Egyptian ruler to agree to free the Jewish people, Moshe's efforts actually caused Pharaoh to stiffen his heart and decree that the Jews be subjected to even harsher labors. So too, after each major plague, Moshe was convinced that *now* he would be able to take his people out of Egypt – only to discover each time, that Pharaoh had changed his mind. And again, Moshe's high hopes came crashing down upon him.

Having led the redemption, Moshe finds himself in the desert desperately trying to quell one rebellion after another. The Jews blame him for all sorts of crimes and corruption, and even demand that he take them back to Egypt! After the debacle with the golden calf, God tells Moshe that He will destroy this people. Moshe must have felt at this point that he had completely failed to educate his people. "What kind of leader, teacher and rabbi am I if I could not even guide my congregation away from worshipping idols?"

Moshe manages to forestall tragedy, but later, after he sends emissaries to "spy" out the land, God decrees that he and the nation will have to walk around in circles for another 39 years! On another occasion, Moshe's tribesmen, led by Korach, attempt a coup that nearly undermines his authority and threatens his life. And then there is the great fiasco whereby Moshe ignores God's exact instructions, and strikes a stone rather than speaking to it in order produce water. Consequently, God gives him the devastating news that he will never be allowed to enter the land of Israel, thus dashing Moshe's ultimate dream of completing the redemption.

What was Moshe's secret? How was he able to continue in the face of so much failure and disappointment? What about Moshe kept him going forward when lesser men would have quit?

The answer is simple: Just like a paratrooper, Moshe knew how to fall without getting hurt, so he could get up quickly and keep moving towards his objectives. He had faith that his failures were just the foundation stones of his future successes. With that in mind, he was always able to get back on his feet and continue the fight.

A famous Yiddish expression says, *He who lies on the ground cannot fall.* Before criticizing another's public defeats, one must always consider how he got himself into a position to fail! Only those special people who set their goals high and climb for the summit, can fall hard. Moreover, those who never fail, never accomplish, since defeat is a necessary step in the process of success. The famous American philosopher Paul Tillich once remarked: "The awareness of the ambiguity of one's highest achievements as well as one's deepest failures is a definite symptom of maturity."

Above all, a person must ask himself what *real* success is all about. Let us draw an example from the world of fitness centers. This site consists of a large hall filled with many pieces of equipment that could be used to take us on long journeys. There are bicycles that go nowhere, no matter how hard and how long we peddle. There are rowing boats but no water, skis without snow, and even climbing frames on which you can climb for hours without getting any higher. Still, you will find lots of perfectly rational people in fitness centers working extremely hard to go nowhere! More remarkably, this sisyphisian futility does not depress them in the least. In fact many return day after day. The reason for this, is, of course obvious: Success with exercise equipment is not measured by how far you go, but how much you change your *self*. Even if externally, there seems to be no success whatsoever, cardiovascularly, *inwardly,* the person on the bike improves his fitness tremendously.

A person who looks only superficially may draw the conclusion that the cyclist, the mountain-climber, and the rower are all complete failures. The wise man smiles and knows that they are in fact, great winners.

20

Moshe and Yitro, Major or Minor in Jurisprudence?

As is well known, Yitro, Moshe Rabeinu's father-in-law, advised him to reform the juridical process used to mete out justice for the Jewish people during their travels in the desert on their way to the land of Israel:

"And it came to pass on the morrow that Moshe sat to judge the people and the people stood around Moshe from the morning until the evening. And Moshe's father-in-law saw all that he did for the people and he said: "What is this that you do to the people...?" And Moshe answered his father in law: "Because the people come to me to inquire of God. If they are solicitous about any matter they come to me. I have to judge between one and the other. I have to make the laws of God and His teachings known."

"And Moshe's father-in-law said unto him: "That what you do is not good. You shall surely wear yourself out and the people that are with you, for this thing is too heavy for you alone, you are not able to carry it out. Hearken unto me...you shall appoint out of all the people able men...and place them over them [the Israelites], leading judges out of thousands and leading judges out of hundreds, leading judges out of fifties and leading judges out of tens. And let these judge the people at all times and it shall be that every major matter will be brought to you but every minor matter they [the other judges] shall judge...."[1]

It is generally believed that Moshe implemented Yitro's program of reforms and indeed appointed judges to hear the smaller cases, freeing Moshe to involve himself only in the major ones. However, a careful reading of the text reveals that this is not entirely true. It seems that Moshe was not prepared to take his father-in-law's suggestions at face

---

[1] *Shemot* 18:13–23.

value – that in fact, he saw some flaws in Yitro's approach. When we dig a little deeper into the way the Torah describes how Moshe implemented changes in the national judicial structure, we see a most significant difference between Moshe and Yitro's attitudes in regard to the application and the function of the law.

When Yitro suggests changes in the juridical process he makes a distinction between a major case (*davar hagadol*) and a minor case (*davar hakaton*). However, when Moshe puts these recommendations into practice, he makes a distinction between a *hard* case (*davar hakasheh*) and a minor case (*davar hakaton*):

"And they [the judges] judged the people at all times; the **hard** case *(davar hakashe)* they brought to Moshe and the minor case *(davar hakaton)* they judged themselves."[2]

Various commentators explain that there is a vast difference between what Yitro calls a *major* case and what Moshe calls a *hard* case.

Yitro considered a *major* case to be one involving, for example, a large sum of money. Consequently, in Yitro's proposal, Moshe would only judge high-stakes, "headline" cases in which substantial amounts of money or property were at issue, while minor monetary disputes would be heard by the judges in the "lower" courts.

Moshe seems to object to this vision for the judicial system. In his eyes a "major case" is one that is harder to judge because of the more complicated and difficult legal principles involved, or because of the subtlety of the distinctions the judge would need to make in order to decide correctly. Obviously then, a so-called major case could have an enormous amount of money or a paltry sum on the line. A problem related to a small amount of money can sometimes cause a judge more juridical hardship – forcing him to draw upon more of his wisdom and experience – than disputes over larger amounts of money.

Jewish Law and Ethics view the quantity of money at stake as completely inconsequential to the rabbinical court's dealings with

---

[2] 18:26.

81

monetary cases. Justice is (or at least tries to be) absolute, while money is relative. What the rich man sees as a mere trifle is a fortune in the eyes of the poor. No objective distinctions between major and minor can be made on the basis of quantities.

Yitro, whose suggestions in part reflected the materialistic ideology of his idolatrous society, could not (yet) fully grasp the notion that "having" more in no way implies "being" more. Moshe Rabeinu, who never for a moment considered that he should give his time and wisdom only to the wealthiest members of the B'nei Yisrael, allowed his father-in-law the honor of restructuring the Jewish nation's juridical procedures, but at the same time, without even mentioning it, he radically altered the intent and content of Yitro's program of reforms. In many ways Moshe's response demonstrates the way Jewish wisdom is meant, more generally, to interact with the world at large. Its purpose is not always to replace other systems, which are many times socially beneficial and highly effective, but rather to refine and elevate these systems in the moral dimension.

21

The Protest of a *Bracha*

In our contemporary world surprise is a rare commodity indeed. Our educational system (with some exceptions) has taught for many decades that everything must make rational sense. Scientific knowledge with its emphasis on order and consistency, together with the study of human behavior and its insistence on universal psychological patterns, have convinced us that there is basically no place for astonishment.

While many of us still live with the "primitive" reality of surprise, this, we are certain, is merely the unhappy product of our limited understanding and knowledge of our world. With a more complete set of data, every phenomenon would become a readily predictable consequence of its causal factors.

The rigid belief in a purely scientific world – defined by unceasing order and consistency – cages our hearts and minds. At the top of the ivory tower, however, scientists are increasingly finding themselves forced to confront the inescapable mysterium behind all existence. Nonetheless, the average human being is still entranced and sedated by the delusion that all is understood and "under control."

The desire to escape the *mysterium tremendum* has naturally led to a secularization of even the most intelligent people's world-views. Convincing themselves that the laws of nature somehow explain "the above and beyond" in totally rational terms, they fail to recognize that these postulates are purely descriptive, and thus completely lack the power to explain anything outside the system they describe. The perception of frequently recurring patterns and phenomena – the basis for establishing the laws of nature – can never be considered a final elucidation. Induction is indeed a powerful tool, because it allows us to make reasonable predictions, which is quite useful given that much of our experience is in fact regular and consistent. However, science can never give us any insight into the ultimate "whys." Why are the laws of nature as they are? Why are we here to ask these questions at all?

As philosophers of science have constantly emphasized, science does not involve itself in ontology, epistemology, or that which is beyond what can be immediately experienced.

Religion in general and the Jewish tradition in particular, warn us against intellectual stagnation. It teaches us that we must be able to appreciate novel insights in repeated, common experiences. There is no greater threat to man's spiritual condition than creating categories and stereotypes that render encounters with the extraordinary mundane, and allow us to feel that everything is readily understandable. The art in a spiritual life, is to recognize the unprecedented in that which is utterly commonplace.

With this in mind, the Jewish sages introduced the practice of saying a *bracha* (blessing) before we eat, drink, and involve ourselves in many religious or even "common" deeds. All such human activities can become spiritually hazardous when they cease to provoke astonishment. Therefore, with every delicious morsel or refreshing sip we imbibe, we must remind ourselves of the inscrutability of such deeds.

Blessings enable us to capture the transcendent aspects of these experiences and prevent them from becoming imprisoned and lost in a mundane view of reality.

A *bracha*, at its core, is a Hebrew expression of the English phrase: Wow! By saying: *"Baruch Ata..."* – "Blessed are You God [for providing us with]...," we make it clear to God and to ourselves that we have not fallen victim to the trap of the ordinary, and that our hearts are still able to soar beyond the average.

22

The Permanent Preciousness of the "Secular" Jew

We live in a most irreverent age. Debunking has become a national pastime, and wherever we turn we find people trying to reveal the clay feet of history's greatest figures. Though we hear it mentioned frequently in speeches, human dignity has become a farce in practice. Instead of deliberately looking for opportunities to love our fellow men as required by our holy Torah, many have rewritten this golden rule for themselves to read: "Distrust your fellow man as you distrust yourself." Our chronic self-judgment and insecurity overflow into our relationships with our fellow men. We fear the mediocrity that resides within us, and so we deceive ourselves into thinking that there are no great spiritual masters left – that we are a generation of spiritual orphans.

This sad condition has even infiltrated into the subconscious of some people in religious communities, although in a more subtle form. Influenced by the irreverent worldview of the host culture, many sincerely religious people, who should know enough to feel a sense of deep respect and love for their neighbors, have unknowingly fallen victim to the debunking epidemic. This worrisome situation exists both within the land of Israel and in the Diaspora.

Observing even those who are fully committed to helping their fellow Jews find their way back to Judaism, we frequently witness an attitude that is actually quite foreign to religious life and thought. Without denying their sincere love for their fellow Jews, and the sacrifices they make in order to connect them to the Torah, we cannot escape the impression that in many instances these well-meaning people "talk down" to the secular Jews they hope to help.

Their need to cure the secular person of his shallow and meaningless lifestyle, lays the foundation for inevitable failure; for such an approach is inherently built on arrogance. In seeing himself as "the ideal" in this situation, the religious Jew turns his secular counterpart into a second-class member of the Jewish people. When confronted with the religious Jew's haughty posture, based on a notion of contrast and his lack of affinity, the secular Jew will always feel inferior. It goes without saying that it is impossible to bring Jews closer to Torah by degrading them. Too many times, well-intentioned attempts to help secular Jews serve only to turn them away from religious people and a religious lifestyle.

When teaching the uninitiated about Judaism, one must keep the suggestion that "one should throw oneself into a burning furnace rather then insult another person publicly"[1] always in the forefront of his mind, and thus be careful not to treat any human being as inferior.

For Jews to bring their brothers and sisters back to Judaism we must rather celebrate the *mitzvot* that they *do* manage to observe. We should do our utmost to find and focus on the positive, and not to dwell on a person's failure to keep all the *mitzvot*. *The foundation should be humility, not arrogance.* There is little doubt that most secular Jews, whether consciously or merely by happenstance, keep a great number of the Torah's commandments. Particularly in the realms of charity and other *mitzvot* concerning the interactions between man and man, secular Jews are generally quite committed to traditional values. We frequently find (despite the absence of ritual practices) within the mindset and lifestyles of many secular Jews the underpinnings of religion: compassion, humility, awe, and in some cases even faith in God. It may be that the minds of religious and non-observant Jews do not fully connect, but their spirits can still touch. Many secular Jews have a deep appreciation of mystery, forgiveness, beauty, and gentleness. Many share an inner faith that God

---

[1] *Berachot* 43b.

cares, and almost all show great contempt for fraud, double standards, and theft – all of which express the deepest religious values.

The first step is to make the so-called irreligious Jew aware of the fact that he is much more religious than he realizes. The best way to call Jews back to their roots is by showing them that they never really left. We must be the ones to point out that God's light still shines on their faces. Once religious Jews integrate the fact that non-observant Jews are their equals, and not their inferiors, a large-scale return to Judaism *on the right terms* will come about.

One of our ancestors' tragic failures was their indifference to the ten tribes of Israel, who were carried away by the Assyrian army after the destruction of the Northern Kingdom. Forgotten by their fellow Jews, they were consigned to oblivion and ultimately vanished.

At this particular moment in Jewish history, every religious Jew should feel a constant sense of terror that we – like those before us who witnessed the nightmare of the Ten Tribes – will remain unaware of our dereliction of duty, and thus cause a tragic failure of epic proportions.

23

Of Rabbinical Courage

One People, Two Worlds:
A Reform Rabbi and an Orthodox Rabbi Explore the Issues That Divide Them
by Amiel Hirsch and Yosef Reinman[1]

"The ultimate measure of a man is not where he stands in a moment of
comfort and convenience,
but where he stands in times of challenge and controversy."
–Martin Luther King, Jr.

This famous statement by Martin Luther King came to mind when I read
One People, Two Worlds by Rabbis Yosef Reinman and Ammiel Hirsch.
This book contains a candid and provoking dialogue about the
fundamental differences between Orthodox and Reform Judaism. Rabbi
Reinman is a member of the hareidi[2] community in Lakewood, New
Jersey, and Rabbi Hirsch is affiliated with the reform community in New
York City.

Educators and many laymen anticipated this book's arrival for
many years. It was a welcome relief to finally find two rabbinic leaders
with the courage to leave their comfort zones in order to engage in a
respectful, but nonetheless head-on confrontation about a wide range of

---

[1] *One People, Two Worlds: A Reform Rabbi And Orthodox Rabbi Explore the Issues That Divide Them.* Ammiel Hirsch and Yosef Reinman, Schocken Books, New York, 2002.

[2] Hareidi literally means pious; however, it is most often used in reference to "ultra-orthodox" Jewish communities, which can be misleading.

topics that touch on the foundations of Jewish belief. This encounter had special significance, for it is a very rare occurrence for a hareidi rabbi to publicly befriend a reform rabbi, and for a reform rabbi to put his antagonism towards the so-called "ultra–orthodox" aside in order to *listen* to what an "ultra-orthodox" rabbi has to say.

While both authors often fail to express their positions in a convincing way, the book is in many ways an eye-opener. From an orthodox perspective it gives a valuable insight into reform ideology. The two rabbis' discourse unveils the many misconceptions that the reform movement has about traditional Judaism, but also manages to convey a biting and honest critique of orthodox thought and practice. The latter contribution could really be a great blessing if orthodox thinkers use it as a catalyst to re-state their beliefs in more profound and accessible ways. After all, the impetus to grow and improve frequently comes not from those who agree with our ideas, but from those who differ and therefore challenge us to sharpen our minds. The Rambam advises in his famous treatise, *Shemonah Perakim*, "Accept the truth from whomever says it."

The book could also be of tremendous benefit to outreach professionals as it contains valuable information about the mindset of the reform world – its problems, its struggles with faith, and its many weaknesses and inconsistencies. Hopefully, the book will also, once and for all, put an end to the claim that all reform rabbis and leaders are seeking deliberately to destroy Judaism and the Jewish People.

Since most reform Jews would not open a book written solely by an orthodox thinker, *One People, Two Worlds* offers a glimpse into orthodox ideology to which a large segment of the Jewish people would never otherwise be exposed. As such the book is a great vehicle for many non-affiliated Jews to learn about the orthodox world's profound spirituality, commitment, and deep religiosity.

It is therefore most disappointing that while a number of leading hareidi rabbis gave encouragement to this venture, many members of the orthodox leadership condemned the book and advised us to remove it from our homes.

Let us read the wise words of Rabbi Judah Lowe Ben Bezalel, the holy Maharal of Prague, one of the great leaders and thinkers of orthodox (hareidi) Judaism in the 16th century:

"It is proper, out of love of reason and knowledge, that you do not [summarily] reject anything that opposes your own ideas, especially so if [your adversary] does not intend merely to provoke you, but rather to declare his beliefs. And even if such [beliefs] are opposed to your own faith and religion, do not say to your opponent: "Speak not and close your mouth." If that happens there will take place no purification of religion. On the contrary, you should say at such times, "Speak up as much as you want, say whatever you wish, and do not say later that had you been able to speak, you would have replied further." For one who causes his opponent to hold his peace and refrain from speaking demonstrates [thereby] the weakness of his own religious faith.... This is therefore the opposite of what some people think – namely, that when you prevent someone from speaking against religion, that strengthens religion. That is not so, because curbing the words of an opponent in religious matters is naught but the curbing and enfeebling of religion [itself]...."[3]

Should we perhaps argue that if we allow our "adversary" to state his beliefs, he might be able to persuade us, or our fellow Jews, to adopt his views; or convince us that *his* is also a legitimate approach to Judaism?

How uplifting and refreshing is the Maharal's suggestion that we should in fact look for the *strongest* opponent to challenge us:

"When a powerful man seeks out an opponent in order to demonstrate his [own] strength, he very much wants his opponent to exercise as much power as he can, so that if he defeats him his own

---

[3] Maharal: *Be'er HaGolah,* end of last chapter. Translations by Rabbi Dr. Norman Lamm: *Torah UMadda,* Jason Aronson, Northvale, New Jersey, London, 1990, pp. 57–58.

victory will be more pronounced. What strength is manifested when the opponent is not permitted to fight?... Hence, one should not silence those who speak against religion...for to do so is an admission of weakness."[4]

Indeed, what kind of message does orthodoxy send its children and students when it shows fear at the prospect of debating people with opposing views? How insecure must the orthodox leadership be regarding the quality of Jewish education that it fears the views of the reform movement? Are orthodox Jews really so vulnerable to reform proselytizing?

It is clear from the outset that Rabbi Reinman's main purpose in agreeing to this debate was to prove that the reform movement is indeed *not* a legitimate expression of authentic Judaism. So if he succeeded, what is the problem? And if the end result is undecided, should the reader not be given the opportunity to decide for themselves? True, there may be readers who read the arguments with a preconceived agenda and thereby arrive at the wrong conclusions, but this is beyond our control. In any event, a person can just as easily misunderstand the Torah, Talmud, Prophets, Midrashim, and their commentaries, with tragic consequences as well. Nothing in this world comes without risk. The great paradox of courage is that one sometimes needs to risk his life in order to save it.

To have arguments in our study halls is easy, since we have only to answer ourselves and not the "adversary." The real test of our beliefs, and our ability to convey them, comes when we are forced to defend and explain them in a context of hostile opposition. For truly great souls, great quarrels are great emancipations, and if anything is desperately needed today it is for orthodoxy to show that it can put up a good fight. "The best way I know of winning an argument is to start by being in the right," Lord Hailsham once said.

The greatest problem with the condemnation hurled at *One People, Two Worlds*, is that it came *after* the book was already published. To call

---

[4] Ibid.

for the removal of a book from the shelves is far more disruptive than simply trying to prevent its publication from the beginning. Bans always drive up sales, and furthermore, the secular world inevitably sees these public outcries as a manifestation of weakness on the part of orthodoxy, which then shines a positive light on the so-called "open mindedness" of reform.

Orthodoxy must wake up and once more challenge the world as Avraham Avinu and so many other great Jews did after him. *Authentic* orthodoxy has nothing to fear. It has all the necessary ingredients to assert itself heroically with great self-confidence. The orthodox leadership should feel free to show unprecedented courage. The case for true Torah Judaism should be made so strongly that reform leaders will be made to question whether or not to remove books from *their* shelves!

Let us hope and pray that Rabbi Reinman and like-minded hareidi rabbis who endorsed this endeavor will respectfully persist with the courage to prove God's utterly compelling and uncompromising path.

24

Surround Yourself with Art and Beauty

So many people fail to appreciate the profound positive impact that nature's beauty can have on the lives of those who take the time to marvel at it. Even many devout individuals, while impressive in their commitment to Torah and *Mitzvot*, do not instill their children with a sense of wonderment for the elegance and grace found in God's world: majestic mountains, lakes, forests, flowers, colorful birds, etc. Related and parallel to this phenomenon, we also perceive a widespread lack of appreciation for art and music. Religious school systems give little if any consideration to these matters, nor are they prioritized in most observant homes. This is a worrisome development, as this aesthetic apathy contradicts, in many ways, the very spirit of authentic Judaism.

Natural beauty, art, and music exist to disturb. Their purpose is to awaken in a sense of wonder in people; and while beauty, art, and music facilitate that wonder, the role of religion is to provide us with the means to respond to it.

Artistic expression and religious observance are both forms of protest against taking the world for granted. The perception of objects as beautiful is an unexplainable phenomenon, and any attempts to rationalize the concept of beauty will be doomed to fail. The same is true for musings on the definition of "art," which belongs to a world beyond words. Real art does not reproduce the visible but rather reveals the invisible. Consequently not even artists are able to explain the inner beauty that resides within their creations. In fact, good artists are usually shocked by the work they produce. In general, they cannot explain their art any more than a plant can explain horticulture. This failure of the rational mind to categorize and define, puts man in direct confrontation with the ineffable, and warns him not to fall victim to the simplistic belief that science can give him any insight into the mystery of our existence. As such, natural beauty and art can be conducive to religious awakening.

And so too music. Music, in its most rarefied forms, is a means of giving form to our inner feelings, and consequently, can help us get in touch with the mystery of our internal worlds. Man is charged with the duty to stand in awe of God's creation. Beauty then, is a tremendous kindness that God did for us, as it renders our task of appreciating His work both easy and immensely pleasurable.

A student once asked the great rabbi, Samson Raphael Hirsch, why in his old age he suddenly decided to spend some time in Switzerland. In his humble way Rabbi Hirsch responded, "As an old man, I am afraid that when I will have to appear in front of the Lord of the Universe in the world to come, He will ask me, 'Samson Raphael! Did you see My mountains in Switzerland?' And I will not know what to answer."[1]

The Talmud adds another dimension to our understanding of the role and importance of aesthetics: "A beautiful wife, a beautiful dwelling place and beautiful furnishings broaden the mind of man."[2] Probably this statement relates to another remark by the sages, "The world needs both spice dealers and tanners – but blessed is he who is a dealer in spices, and woe unto him whose trade is tanning [because of the unpleasant odors produced in the tanning process].[3]

Concerning music we are told that "David took the harp and played with his hand, and Shaul (the first King of Israel) was relieved and well and the bad spirit left him."[4] Furthermore, the sages must have had good reason to inform us that the Temple service involved a choir of

---

[1] Rabbi Samson Rafael Hirsch, *Architect of Torah Judaism for the Modern World*, Eliyahu Meir Klugman, Artscroll, NY, 1996, p. 320.
[2] *Berachot* 57b.
[3] *Pesachim* 65a.
[4] *II Shmuel* 16:25.

Levites who filled God's House with other-worldly music and song. Many *Tehillim* (Psalms) begin with the phrase, "Lamnatzeach Bin'ginoth," which Rabbi Samson Raphael Hirsch translates as, "To Him who grants spiritual victory through the art of music."[5]

The sages made a number of remarkable observations concerning beauty. The Torah[6] commands that the urban planners in Israel should be certain to leave 1000 ell of untilled land around each city, to allow nature to manifest its beauty. The Mishnah adds that one is allowed to remove all unseemly objects from the vicinity of the city, to ensure that the landscape's appearance will always be pleasing.[7]

The perception of beauty – whether in art, music or nature – can calm us when we are stressed, or inspire our creativity and spur us on to great accomplishments.[8] Jewish education should encourage our children to study and appreciate natural beauty, art, and music. This should be done within the framework of the school and home with emphasis given to the religious significance of the aesthetic experience. With the proper perspective, visiting an art museum, or a walk in the woods can effect real spiritual growth.

It is revealing that the Talmud calls on us to have beautiful furnishings in our homes.[9] While many people do not have the financial means to spend on interior design, many are able, with only a little money, to turn their homes into warm and inviting environments. Few can afford to adorn their walls with original oil paintings, or to walk on expensive Persian rugs. Still, technology allows us to enjoy quality reproductions of even the greatest masterpieces. With an inexpensive frame and some light, one can recreate an ineffable "museum experience" in his living room. Through some simple flower decorations one can

---

5 *Tehillim* 4:1.

6 *Bamidbar* 35:5.

7 *Bava Batra* 2:9.

8 See Rabbi J.L. Bloch, *Shiurei Da'at*, page 194, See also Rabbi D. Katz, *Tenuat HaMussar*, Tel Aviv, 5723, Volume 5, p. 76, et seq.

9 *Berachot* 32a.

completely revitalize an otherwise drab and dreary room. There are infinite possibilities that each person, according to his or her tastes and emotional needs, can easily secure. All that is required is a minimum of attention and a dash of creativity.

To look at a Rembrandt and let its beauty wash over one's mind is not just a sensory delight, but a religious experience that God, in His kindness and wisdom, granted His creatures. Rabbi Avraham Yitzchak Kook, the famous mystic and philosopher who became the Chief Rabbi of what was then called Palestine, was stranded in London during the First World War. As often as he could, he used to visit the National Gallery and look at its Rembrandts. On one of these occasions Rav Kook made a striking observation. The Torah states that God created light on the first day. But He only created the sun and the moon on the fourth day! What then was the source of the light on day one? To this, the sages explain that the first light was really a special Divine radiance that God set apart as a gift for the righteous in the world to come.[10] Rabbi Kook commented that he was certain God granted some of that light to Rembrandt.[11]

Of course, we know that some music, paintings, and photography implicitly conflict with our sense of decency and good taste, and convey messages that directly oppose the Jewish conception of holiness. At its apex, classical art and music has the capacity to make us look beyond the mundane world and perceive the miracle of all existence frozen in an eternal moment or in a heavenly combination of musical notes. Today we are confronted with a lot of artists and musicians whose only goal (motivated largely by a lack of real talent) is to shock. As such, their popularity will necessarily fade away, since each of their pieces can only really shock us once. This does not give us license, however, to

---

[10] See Rashi on *Bereishit* 1:4.
[11] See *From Optimism to Hope*, Jonathan Sacks, Continuum, London, 2004, pp. 29–30.

completely ignore the beauty that does exist within the world of art and music. To refuse to listen to a refined piece of music is to close oneself off from one of the most sublime experiences our world has to offer.

Oliver Wendell Holmes often suggested that a "music-bath" could be of greater benefit to the soul than a water bath is to the body. It is time for the religious community to put this matter back on its agenda.

25

Surround Yourself with Cleanliness:
A Project of Common Interest

"Cleanliness is not next to Godliness nowadays,
for cleanliness is made an essential,
and Godliness is regarded as an offence."
–C.K Chesterton (*On Lying in Bed, Tremendous Trifles*, 1909)

Throughout most of history, religious Jews' hygiene standards were far more advanced than those of most other people. Indeed, Jewish law dating back thousands of years contains a far-reaching codex for personal and environmental cleanliness that would seem novel and forward-thinking to many twenty-first century lawyers, environmentalists, and public health-care workers.

Besides numerous laws that prohibit needless destruction of the natural environment and its resources, as well as pollution in its various forms, Jewish Law also seeks to preserve animal life and maintain clean and pleasant conditions both in the home and in the public domain.

In a fascinating narrative, the Talmud tells of the great Rabbi Huna who asked his son why he was not attending the lectures of Rabbi Chisda, a brilliant, younger colleague. Rabbi Huna's son, in his innocence answered that he wanted "to hear words of Torah and not about worldly matters." Taken aback by this response, Rabbi Huna asked his son which "worldly matters" Rabbi Chisda actually discussed. The son responded that the sage lectured about cleanliness and appropriate behavior in the bathroom. After hearing this, Rabbi Huna exclaimed in wonderment

"Here are matters of life and death [and thus of Torah], and you call them worldly matters!?!"[1]

On another occasion, the Mishna[2] states that "it is not permitted to soak clay in the public highway…. During building operations, stones [and other building materials] must be deposited immediately on the building site [and not left on the road]." The Talmud also forbids other forms of litter, such as dropping bottles in the public domain without picking up the shards of broken glass.[3] The purpose of these laws is to protect the public against injury, and also to ensure a minimum standard of cleanliness in society.

With their keen insight into human nature, the Jewish sages understood the direct impact of these laws on the society's psychological well-being. The Talmud quotes a source that states that if a spring serves as the water supply for two towns, but does not provide sufficient water for both, the town closer to the source takes precedence.[4] The other town, in such a case, would need to find other ways to get sufficient water. However, when it is a choice between the farther town's drinking water and the nearer town's laundry, the farther town's drinking water should come first.[5]

To our surprise, Rabbi Yossi objects to this ruling and states that the closer town's laundry will take priority over the farther town's drinking water! The Talmud, explaining Rabbi Yossi's reasoning, refers to a statement of the famous authority, Shmuel, who says that constantly wearing dirty clothes causes depression and mental instability!

In other words, clean garments are not a luxury. Jewish law considers cleanliness a necessity. The great Halachic authority, Rabbi Ahai Gaon (8th century), ruled that the law is decided according to Rabbi

---

Shabbat 82a.
Bava Metzia 10:5.
Bava Kama 29b.
Nedarim 80b.
For full understanding of this statement see the commentaries on *Nedarim* 80b.

Yossi's opinion.[6] A wealth of similar laws and observations are to be found throughout traditional Jewish literature.

Unfortunately these laws do not seem to be of great concern within many orthodox communities today. Though litter does not pollute the streets of orthodox communities any more so than in secular communities (as certain secular observers would like to claim), one still wonders why rabbis and religious leaders who are so genuinely committed to the Torah and Tradition do not speak out on these issues to ensure that the relevant laws receive the attention they deserve. Indeed, given the spirit of Jewish Law, we would expect that the streets in orthodox neighborhoods would look remarkably cleaner than anywhere else.

By implementing the Torah's laws in this realm – which should really not be too difficult, for after all, we're only talking about throwing garbage in bins rather than in the streets – orthodox communities will take away much of the ammunition in their secular detractors' arsenals, and in so doing, will make a tremendous *kiddush Hashem*, which is in fact the purpose of being a Jew.[7]

---

[6] *She'eltoth: Re'eh* 147.

[7] For further reading on this subject, see the excellent essay by Dr. Manfred Gerstenfeld and Dr. Avraham Wijler: "The Ultra Orthodox Community and Environmental Issues," *Jerusalem Letter/Viewpoints*, no. 415, 21 *Tishrei* 5760, October 1999.

26

Lashon Hara About the World and the Fly in the Bottle

Woody Allen, an unusual but keen observer of our world, once remarked: "More than at any time in history, mankind faces a crossroads. One path leads to despair and utter hopelessness, the other to total extinction. Let us pray that we have the wisdom to choose correctly."

Sometimes it seems that we are surrounded by war, destruction, hunger, and illness – without end and without much hope. Philosophers, scientists, and physicians offer all sorts of solutions, but we continue to witness terrorist attacks in many civilized countries and major disasters in nearly every part of the world; and so we get the impression that in spite of all our efforts to make things better, matters are only getting worse. Every cure we discover is followed by a new and even deadlier disease. Every peace accord gets violated, inviting greater tensions and more destructive scenarios.

This, however, is only a partial picture. These kinds of thoughts emerge from a psychological condition from which many of us suffer. Looking closer, this world view reminds us of *lashon hara* (evil speech) – not about our fellow men, but about our world.

Evil speech arises from a kind of self-distrust rooted in deep psychological insecurities. It is a self-defeating strategy built on an illusion, similar to two elevators that move in opposite directions. The moment that one descends, the people in the other immediately feel that they have started to ascend. So too, by obsessing over and emphasizing the faults of the other, one can begin to feel impeccable by comparison.

The world we inhabit is also a place of much outstanding good. Most people are decent and law-abiding. Billions leave their homes in the morning and return safely every night. Thousands and thousands of planes take off and land every day without the slightest problem. Most children come into the world with strong healthy minds and bodies. The sun rises every day without exception. There is always enough oxygen for everyone. Most people today live by much higher economic standards than our forefathers ever even dreamed of achieving. Pain can be prevented, reduced and eliminated with much greater ease and effectiveness by the medical community than ever before. International communication systems allow us to stay in touch with loved ones wherever we live. Luxurious old age homes have replaced what was once a commonplace tragedy of elderly people dying in the streets. And on and on.

True, the world is far from ideal. Nevertheless, people seem so eager to look at our globe like we look at white paper with a black ink spot. They see only the blotch and ignore the pristine background. Only the obvious negative space seems worthy of notice. Why is this so?

Let us suggest that this epistemological phenomenon is caused by the fact that the confrontation with goodness generates a certain psychological disturbance. Exposure to Good forces us to contemplate the meaning of our lives, because the beauty in the good touches our souls. About goodness we cannot complain; we can only contemplate. And this embarrasses us, because we do not want to accept the outcome of our meditations. Nor do we feel adequate to respond to the moral and religious demands that Good and Beauty make, as they remind us that our lives have a purpose.

So we hide, dig in, and create a sophisticated defense mechanism. We make sure that we do not get exposed – consciously – to all the beauty. We focus on the black spot and deny the white paper. And we have plenty of company. Our media constantly shines their lights on disasters and disease. Everyone knows that we need much more balanced reporting, but this becomes just another target for complaint. We know we would not really bother to read stories about do-gooders and all their good deeds. That would be too dangerous.

Instead we speak *lashon hara* about our world. We give it a bad name so we can feel secure about where we are physically and spiritually. "Life is hard enough. We can barely survive. How could we possibly indulge in meaning?" We force the elevator of this world to descend so we can feel ourselves rising, as we, in truth, maintain our comfortable mediocrity.

Part of the purpose of a genuinely religious lifestyle is to free us from dependence on this illusion. It is not that religion shows us something entirely new. It merely shows us how to look properly at what we see.

The message is clear: After all is said and done, there is dazzling goodness in this world. Overwhelmingly, order reigns over chaos. We live amongst wondrous variety to enjoy, and not in a monotony to endure. And, above all, there is the infinite grace of so many beautiful human beings and their deeds.

The great Austrian philosopher, Ludwig Wittgenstein, once remarked that the average person lives like a fly trapped in a bottle. The fly keeps banging itself against the glass. The more it tries, the more it flounders, until it finally drops in exhaustion. Its failure, of course, is only that it forgets to look up.

27

"Es Past Nicht" and Jewish Pride

A certain British politician once chided Benjamin Disraeli, the Earl of Beaconsfield (1804–1881), about being Jewish. "Indeed," he responded, "I am a Jew; and when the ancestors of the right honorable gentleman were brutal savages on an unknown island, mine were priests in the Temple of Solomon."

In these difficult days for the State of Israel, and the increase of anti-Semitic invective spouted by leaders across the globe, we must gird ourselves by taking Disraeli's response to heart.

The famous Chassidic master, Rabbi Nachman of Breslov once said, "In remembering, lies the secret of redemption." This, indeed, is a crucial message for all Jews under siege. From the recognition of our unrivaled past, we should be able to draw the strength to confront our enemies and build a glorious future in spite of them. Moshe Rabeinu taught us this secret as just before our ancestors entered the land of Israel: "Remember the days of old; consider the generations long past. Ask your father and he will tell you, your elders and they will explain to you."[1]

Moshe sent a strong message to all Jews living in all future generations that they will only be able to hold onto their land as long as they remain intimately connected to their history, so they will always stay conscious of the reason for their existence.

Indeed the Jews have more history than any other nation, and it is a history of quality, not of quantity. We Jews do not pay homage to the heroic deeds of gladiators or the astonishing victories of armies, but rather to the soaring moral accomplishments of individual men and

---

[1] *Devarim* 32:7.

women of faith who made this humble people into God's chosen nation. While we often fought physical battles to ensure our survival, we never lost sight of the fact that existence would be meaningless if not for the nation's spiritual purpose. Our people's exalted ethical standards and spirituality were always the source of our pride and honor, and without question, our most valuable national treasure.

The Gentile author, Lyman Abbott, once wrote, "We gentiles owe our life to Israel. It is Israel who brought us the message that God is one.... It is Israel who in bringing us the divine law, has laid the foundation of liberty.... It is Israel who brought us our Bible, our prophets and our apostles...."[2]

The French historian Leroy Beaulieu added that, "As compared with the Jews, we are young, we are new-comers; in the matter of civilization they are far ahead of us. It was in vain that we locked them up for several hundred years behind the walls of the ghetto. No sooner were their prison gates unbarred than they easily caught up with us even on those paths which we had opened up without their aid."[3]

When observing world Jewry's spiritual condition and the general atmosphere in the State of Israel today, we find so many Jews who have forgotten who they are and what their mission in the world is all about. It is as if they have lost their past. More and more they have given up remembering and as a consequence of their indifference to their roots, they render the idea of redemption nearly impossible. In many secular Israeli schools, Israel's exalted spiritual past is scoffed at and only considered in the context of a purely academic study of Jewish antiquity. Meanwhile, Israeli society desperately searches for its raison d'être in technology, secular academia, and the attempt to generate a flourishing economy. But the more the secular culture achieves its goals, the less solid ground remains under its feet.

---

[2] Quoted in Rabbi J.H. Hertz, *A Book of Jewish Thoughts*, Oxford University Press, London, 1917, 1966.
[3] Ibid.

Long before other nations had the words to speak about re-discovering their "roots," Jews understood that there is no reason for survival into the future without a clearly defined mission. No people's mission can survive without the belief in the importance of the goal and uniqueness of those who seek to achieve it, both of which derive their life-force from the original "root experiences" of the past.

The secular call for extreme tolerance and assimilation, so often heard ringing in the halls and lecture rooms of Israel's universities, will, if heeded, ultimately put an end to Israel's meaningful existence. Only in the actualization and expression of one's uniqueness is one most able to contribute to others, because only then does a person possess something special to share. The pride we should feel about our unique heritage should not inflate our sense of importance or serve as a reason to demand greater privileges, nor should it motivate the creation of a nation of "blue-blooded" elitists. On the contrary, when a Jew truly knows who he is, he will feel a tremendous sense of obligation and responsibility to the rest of the world.

There is a powerful expression in Yiddish: "Es past nicht," which means that "It does not suit a Jew to do such things." Because a proud Jew feels that he must develop himself in order to be of real value in the nation's quest to accomplish its divine mission of being a light to the nations, certain deeds become abhorrent in his eyes. A Jew does not feel burdened by this self-control. He enjoys it, because his discipline and the dignity with which he behaves, emanate from his feelings of pride.

The State of Israel faces more violent crime, more drug addiction, and more domestic abuse than ever before. The pervasive sense of purposelessness in secular society is causing Jews to self-destruct. No legislation or police enforcement can solve this epidemic. Only when the notion of *"Es past nicht"* returns to the secular Israeli vocabulary, will there be renewed hope for the nation. Then we will know that the redemption is nigh.

28

Marriage, "Li," and the Need for Martyrdom

The great Chassidic leader Rabbi Menachem Mendel of Kotzk, lamenting Jews' detachment from Judaism, once commented that when a bridegroom stands under the *chupa* (bridal canopy) he can say hundreds of times to his future bride, "You are betrothed," but it is as if he said nothing at all until he adds one more Hebrew word to the formula – "*Li*." "You are betrothed *to me*." Only then do their souls become one. All the family and friends can be present, the musicians playing beautifully, the food served, and the new home waiting and ready – but nothing real happens until the groom utters the word "*Li*." To me.

The crucial word in life is "*Li*" – to me. A person can only generate meaning in his life when he commits himself entirely to a relationship with the Other. Such a commitment must not be partial, but total. "Till death do we part."

The Kotzker Rebbe's observation is perhaps the most crucial message for Jews around the world today. The Jewish community concerns itself with many issues, some of which may even threaten its survival, but so long as Jews remain distanced, un-inspired, and unwilling to say "*Li*" (i.e., to feel a personal and *total* commitment to an authentically Jewish way of life), all the well-intentioned committee meetings and fundraisers will fail to create the conditions necessary for continuity and renewal.

Looking at the state of Jewish commitment today we do see an impressive level of scholarship within the world of academia. Comparative studies of Jewish thought and the ideologies and rituals espoused by other religions, as well as investigations into Jewish history, archaeology, and philological studies keep tens of thousands of brilliant

Jewish students intellectually engaged in the libraries of the best colleges and universities in the world. Textbooks and magazines publish important articles on questions such as: Are the Jews a race, a cultural entity, or a religious group? But the value of all such studies remains limited if the student's research never bring him to a point at which he feels compelled to add the word "*Li*" – "to me." Studying Judaism without any personal connection to the material is analogous to studying Man as a mere collection of cells, while ignoring the human being's unique inner essence; that within man reside tremendous emotional and spiritual dimensions that define his true nature.

Jewish studies in academic circles may make contributions to the sum total of knowledge about our people and our past, but they fail to even touch upon the most important aspects of human existence, which are the very aspects that Judaism comes to address: What does it mean to be human? What is the purpose of our existence? What is our task and mission in this world, and how can we elevate ourselves to attain a measure of dignity? Such questions involve our whole being. They are the ultimate "*Li*" issues, and they should haunt us until we have no escape.

What value is there in all this scholarship if it stays on such a superficial level, and never scratches the surface of what it means to be a Jew? Noting similarities between Jewish festivals and the holidays of other faiths may be an interesting way to pass the time, but to do so at the expense of recognizing Judaism's spiritual relevance – that part of our wisdom tradition that offers answers to the most important questions – is tragic. Where so many Jewish academics falter is in their attempts to hide from the crucial "*Li*."

To understand what it means to be a Jew, one must *surpass* the purely intellectual element of these studies and embrace their broader implications. To be a Jew means being a messenger, to be an eager and proud servant of God, ready to teach the rest of Mankind the art of morality and spiritual transformation, and to feel utter *dis*-satisfaction at merely being "civilized." Jewishness is about accessing and encountering our deepest, most cherished, and most transcendent emotions. Jewishness means that instead of feeling bored with life, we feel constantly surprised by the depth and strength of our character. Just like great works of art, Judaism does not produce, but rather *inspires,* unanticipated insights and the deepest forms of authentic self-expression.

The tragedy of the Jewish world today is that too many Jews lack the courage to confront their inner Jewishness. They are too happy to coldly observe the Jewish people and Judaism as sociological phenomena to be examined from *without.* They hold themselves at a distance so that they never get to hear the music that resounds *within* Judaism, and then they complain that this music is absent from their religion. It is like the music student who takes his violin, disassembles it, studies the strings and the polished wood, and then complains that he cannot find the music and so concludes that it must be a fake.

"*Li.*" means picking up a bow and playing such sweet sounds, until the tears literally pour from one's eyes in rapture. But Jews will first need to recognize that our people has a singular and distinctive contribution to make to the world. If we fail to develop and cultivate our uniqueness then our people will suffer, and the whole world will lose out as well.

At the end of his famous essay "Two Concepts of Liberty," the late British philosopher, Sir Isaiah Berlin, tries to convince us that one needs "to realize the relative validity of one's convictions and yet stand for them unflinchingly."[1] We must agree with Michael Sandel's obvious and biting critique when he states, "If one's convictions are only relatively valid, why stand for them unflinchingly?"[2] Indeed, this kind of liberalism, with all its inclusion and tolerance, keeps the *"Li"* fenced outside of our

---

[1] Isaiah Berlin, *Liberty,* Oxford Press, Oxford, 2002, p. 217.
[2] Michael Sandel, *"Liberalism and its Critics,"* Blackwell, Oxford, 1984, p. 8.
*Both of the above sources are quoted in Chief Rabbi Jonathan Sacks's fine work: *"The Dignity of Difference: How to Avoid the Clash of Civilizations,"* Continuum, London, NY, p. 18.

lives, and turns us into spectators looking into our inner world like visitors at the zoo who wave to the caged gorillas.

Albert Camus once said, "There is only one serious philosophical problem, and that is suicide." The great Jewish thinker Abraham Joshua Heschel disagreed. It is not suicide but martyrdom, he said, which is our only real problem: *Is there anything worth dying for?*

This is indeed the ultimate question for Jews today. When Jews will stop observing passively and start actively living Judaism again, they will realize that their Jewishness is even worth dying for.

To Marry, to Buy, and the Future of Israel

From an extraordinary statement in the Talmud, we get a glimpse into the utter despair that gripped our sages after they witnessed the destruction of the Temple, the murder of millions of Jews, and the complete breakdown of Jewish life in the ancient land of Israel.

"By right we should issue a decree that Jews should not marry and have children so that the seed of Avraham will come to an end on its own accord."[1] No other statement could better express total despondency. The small remnant of the once glorious nation of Israel were exiled from the land and forced to live as refugees among violent, anti-Semitic societies, and thus the sages concluded that there was no hope for a better future. Why continue to suffer when fading into oblivion could be the people's last possible salvation?

Still – the Talmud reports – the simple Jews of this dark era of Jewish history refused to succumb to their leaders' dejection. Instead, they decided to rebuild Jewish life to the best of their abilities in spite of their adverse circumstances. This will to go on demonstrated courage of an unprecedented dimension. Without country, army, or finances, and surrounded by millions whose hatred for Jews was only too well-known, these Jews found the strength to get married and raise families. Despite the total collapse of Jewish life as they knew it, they opted for the seemingly impossible.

In a similar vein, the book of Yirmiyahu (chapter 32) tells the story of the Babylonian siege of Jerusalem. After three years, the Babylonian army successfully cut off the Jews' supply lines and famine spread throughout the city. Simultaneously, a number of deadly plagues

---

[1] *Bava Batra* 60b.

afflicted the Jews and claimed hundreds of thousands of victims. When Yirmiyahu, the "calamity prophet," predicted the city would soon fall and that the king himself would be captured, King Zedekiyahu threw him in jail.

While in the dungeon, and to his utter surprise, God appeared to Yirmiyahu and told him to buy a piece of land near Jerusalem from his cousin Hananel. Only a moment later Hananel indeed appeared and suggested that Yirmiyahu should buy this piece of land. Consequently, the prophet signed a contract with his cousin and buried the document in the ground to preserve it from the inevitable onslaught of destruction. Then he announced, "For this is what the Lord Almighty, the God of Israel, says: "Houses, fields and vineyards will again be bought in the land.""[2]

How utterly astonishing that under the disastrous circumstances in which he found himself, one simple Jew had the nerve to pitch a property deal to the *very* prophet who persistently prophesized that total catastrophe was imminent! Never mind that this piece of land was most likely littered with corpses and situated in the middle of a war zone such that its new buyer could not even think of going to visit his investment. Who would ever think of trying to sell, let alone buy in such a market?

Indeed, it is not Yirmiyahu who plays the role of hero in this small vignette, but rather his low-profile cousin Hananel. After all, God explicitly instructed Yirmiyahu to buy the land, so how could he refuse? But from where did Hananel derive the courage even to suggest such a ludicrous transaction?

Nothing would stop Hananel from pushing forward with his life. His faith allowed him to buy and sell with the absolute knowledge that one day everything would fall into place, and a beautiful Jewish life would start anew in the land of our forefathers.

---

[2] Ibid, 15.

Today it may be horrible, but in the future there will be joy. This was the unrivaled emunah of Hananel, which even Yirmiyahu the prophet had to acknowledge.

Brit Mila: An Oath of Loyalty[1]

In previous generations, parents arranged marriages for their sons and daughters, convinced that the spouses they chose for their children would be ideal life partners for them. In a similar way, but on a deeper level, Jewish parents today bring their newborn sons into a covenant with the God of Israel, eternally uniting them with their most ideal Partner. Circumcision is the process by which a Jewish child and God get engaged.

.Circumcision is an eternal pledge that parents make to God. It is a promise that their child will not be an ordinary human being, but one who will live by God's commandments and will consequently help guide Mankind towards the final redemption. By arranging a *brit mila*, Jewish parents proudly proclaim that their son is destined to become a light and a blessing to all nations.[2] One may want to ask: what gives the parents the right to bring this child into an eternal covenant without his consent? How can we commit a child to a life-long mission that he may not choose to fulfill?

Judaism has a remarkable table-turning response to this argument. Should we not wonder whether it is even more unjust to bring a child into the world *without* a higher mission? While Socrates taught us that a life without thinking is not worth living, Judaism teaches us that life without a commitment to God (i.e., without meaning) is no life at all. The dignity of man stands in proportion to his obligations. We pass on this divine dignity to our children when we make them contractually obligated to fulfill God's covenant. To shield them from this most awesome

---

[1] Inspired by Abraham Joshua Heschel.
[2] *Bereishit* 12:8.

responsibility is to deny them the opportunity to experience the highest, truest value of living in this world.

The circumcision – this promise – is God's seal, imprinted into human flesh. And it is only proper that this sign of allegiance should be imposed upon the body, for after all, it is not the soul that needs to make a commitment. The soul *is* naturally, fully committed to serving its Creator. It is the body that, because of its inclination to feed only its own base desires and needs, must make a vow to compel itself to serve God. Like a piece of paper that carries the buying power of a certain dollar amount, the body serves as the vessel to transport the soul. Just as the symbolic markings on the bill inform us about the value bestowed to it by the treasury department, so too the "signs" we make on our bodies can reveal the greatness of the souls they house. Furthermore, if the body fails to live up to its lofty responsibilities, the physical imprint of the circumcision serves as a constant reminder of what it means to reside in the presence of God, and as a testimony to one's spiritual obligations and potential.

Like the revelation at Sinai, a circumcision is an event that exists as a moment in the past, and also extends eternally into the present. From man's perspective, the *brit mila* happens just once, but from God's perspective the message conveyed in this act – the Jewish nation's unceasing commitment to God – resounds forever. Monuments of stone may disappear; acts of spirit will never pass away.

At Sinai the Jews committed themselves to the Torah with the words, *Na'ase Ve-Nishma*, "we shall do and we shall hear." Without yet knowing what the Torah would require of them, the Jewish people committed themselves to the uncertain task of serving the Creator of the universe. On the eighth day of the child's life, at the time of circumcision, the newly born child's parents imprint his body with God's seal, and thus bring him into the covenant with God in the tradition of *Na'ase Ve-Nishma*. The child thus begins his journey on a road of commitment to holiness that, although not yet known, is the most challenging and most rewarding mission life can offer – to become a servant of God and a blessing to all nations.

31

Shabbat: The Sanctification and Importance of Time

"This is the burnt offering of the Shabbat on its Shabbat."
—*Bamidbar* 28:10

Rashi asks the question: Why does the Torah need to specify that the Sabbath offering should be brought on Shabbat. If it is called a *Shabbat* offering, then is it not implicit and obvious that it is supposed to be sacrificed on the Shabbat!?

Rashi answers simply that one might have thought that if he forgot to bring this offering on a particular Shabbat, he could still bring it on a subsequent Shabbat (i.e., he would just bring two sacrifices the following week). To make sure that one will not make this mistake, the Torah uses this language to instruct us that we may only bring this sacrifice on its own Shabbat. Once the day has passed that offering is no longer relevant and valid.

Although Jewish Law does allow a person to make up for missed *mitzvot* in certain instances, this is usually only permissible in cases of duress.[1] In a few cases, a person can perform a mitzvah whose time has passed, but only at a *bedi'avad* (a posteriori) level, and not *lechatechila* (a priori).

While the expression "Jewish time" is well known, and suggests a more relaxed attitude towards punctuality, Judaism actually takes time very seriously. The Jewish philosopher Abraham Joshua Heschel *z"l*

---

[1] See for example the case of *Pesach Sheni, Bamidbar* 9:6–13.

explained that Judaism is the art of sanctifying time, and that this is of far greater importance than sanctifying physical space.[2]

Indeed, the Torah first speaks about holiness in relation to time. "And God blessed the seventh day and sanctified it."[3] So too, we know that commencing with Shabbat even a second too late, or ending it even a second too early, violates its sanctity.

The Shabbat protects man from himself. By nature, man keeps himself very busy trying to occupy time and space with his self-expressions. On Shabbat he is asked to cease from this activity and reverse it. He must make space for the rest of creation and for God. As such he must release the reigns he holds over space and time and let them proceed without his intervention. Because he is not allowed to "work" on Shabbat (which includes even transporting objects from one domain to another) a Jew learns how to distance himself from his physical space.

The same is true about time. It is not the Jew who decides when Shabbat begins or ends. God decides, via the orbits of the celestial bodies, the duration of this holy day. As such, man can no longer rule over time. As the Sabbath comes in, a Jew suddenly finds himself in a position to simply appreciate and experience "quality" time.

To set one's schedule around fixed times – for prayers, for meals, for learning, etc. – does not only inject order into one's life, but also meaning; and as such one gains an opportunity to sanctify those moments. The chaos of a week without order, of days without set times, is yet another manifestation of the secularization of society and the profanation of the sacred.

Thus the Torah emphatically tells us to bring the Sabbath sacrifice at its proper time. Matters of importance have to be done promptly and with alacrity. To procrastinate and postpone too often means to profane.

---

[2] *The Sabbath: Its Meaning for Modern Man*, Farrar, Straus and Giroux, NY, 1951.
[3] *Bereishit* 2:3.

32

Rosh Hashana *Teshuva* – A Matter of Seduction

Teshuva, the art of repentance, is far from easy. Not only is it difficult to confront oneself honestly about one's own shortcomings, but it is even more difficult to internalize the need to repent and then transform this into action. How many of us are really capable of reaching such a lofty goal?

Our sages, well aware of these difficulties, looked for ways to pave our road to repentance. One of many suggestions is expressed in a Midrash that refers to the *Haftara* of *Shabbat Shuva*, the Sabbath between Rosh Hashana and Yom Kippur.

In this *Haftara*, taken from the book of Hoshea we read: "Turn, Israel, to the Lord your God, because you have stumbled over your transgressions. *Take with you words and return to God...*"[1] On this verse, *Yalkut Shimoni*, a midrashic commentary, states: "Take with you words, like the words through which you *seduced* God at Sinai when you declared, 'We shall do and we shall hear.'"

"We shall do and we shall hear" was the expression with which the children of Israel, while standing at Sinai, promised to fulfill the *Mitzvot*, stating that they were prepared to commit themselves to God's will, even without knowing the actual contents of the covenant. The words "through which you *seduced* God" are, however, most disturbing. It hints at the idea that this expression of total commitment was not entirely genuine, perhaps even unethical, and thus contrary to Jewish values as we know them.

We are even more surprised when we read that this phraseology refers to Israel's failure to live up to its commitment from the very

---

[1] 14:4.

beginning. Immediately after the words, "We shall do and we shall hear," the Torah informs us that the children of Israel fell victim to one of the most severe transgressions in Jewish history – the creation and worship of the Golden Calf. It seems then that the words, "We shall do and we shall hear," may have been a bit idealistic and perhaps unrealistic. This does not suggest, however, that their original intentions were in any way dishonest. The fact that the Jews were unable to hold up their end of the deal does not necessarily imply bad faith.

The Midrash sees things differently. Seduction is after all a pre-conceived attempt to make an impression that is not entirely true – to present a most favorable, but somewhat false, façade.

What, then, does the *haftara* mean when it suggests that we should use words of seduction at the time of Rosh Hashana and Yom Kippur to aid in the process of *teshuva?* Why should we utter words that are not entirely truthful?

Rabbi Eliyahu Eliezer Dessler, *z"l*, one of the most outstanding thinkers in modern Jewish history, resolves this problem by analyzing the nature of a promise. A promise, states Rabbi Dessler, by definition includes the potential for falsehood. After all, at the time of the promise, the commitment is nothing but words. There is no reality to the statement, since the promise does not relate to what is done now, in the present, but what the parties intend to do in the future. At the moment the promise is made it is still unfulfilled and as such not (yet) true. In this sense, it carries the dimension of a deception, especially since it is always possible that, despite even the best intentions, the promise may never be fulfilled. In spite of the potential downside, making a promise can be of great moral value since it instills in a man an added sense of urgency to make the content of his promise come to fruition. This is the power of a promise. Even though one risks lying and breaking one's word, a promise can inspire us to succeed in the most difficult and important realms of life.[2]

---

[2] *Michtav Mi'Eliahu*, Book 4, Section on *Teshuva*.

Progress throughout human history was made largely because people committed themselves with promises that they then felt compelled to actualize. As the famous saying attests: "We promise much as to avoid giving little."[3]

We now may start to understand the Midrash. The only way Israel was able to force itself to a commitment to live by the demands of the Torah was by making a promise: "We shall do and we shall hear." At the time they made this commitment, they knew that it came with the possibility of eventually violating the treaty. And so we see the degree of deception involved when nearly a moment afterwards, the Jewish people turned their backs on God to worship the Golden Calf in His stead! This, however, does not mean that they were wrong to enter into the covenant. The obligations they took on with their utterance – "We shall do and we shall hear" – carried the seeds of success, even if at the time they made the promise they were not 100% genuine. Their higher-order value was to fulfill the covenant, and so they committed themselves in the hopes that their lower order values would eventually come into line with what they knew to be the right way to live.

God, consequently, asks the Jews and all of mankind, during times of introspection, such as on Rosh Hashana and Yom Kippur, to use words of seduction. Even though these words will not always come true, without them we don't even give ourselves the chance for success.

Hoshea's suggestion to "take with you words [of seduction] and turn to God" is, therefore, of profound value. Even when we are not fully committed to *teshuva* (repentance) at the time of the High Holidays, we should at least utter those words of *teshuva*, since it may come to pass at a later date that we will feel an honest desire to live up to our commitments and actually repent. In the promise lies the potential for our spiritual elevation and salvation, and for this reason God suggests that we should try and seduce Him, just like our forefathers did at Sinai (and also seduce ourselves, to greater growth and spirituality). Thus let us

---

[3] Vauvenargues, *Reflections and Maxims*, p. 436

all pronounce the words, "We shall do and we shall hear," during the High Holidays.[4]

---

[4] The *ba'alei mussar*, the great teachers of Jewish ethics, suggest that one should not keep such promises private, but make them in the company of one's spouse, children and friends so as to secure their fulfillment. Nobody likes to show himself as untrustworthy before one's fellow men.

33

Rosh Hashana and Yom Kippur:
The Celebration of the Human Deed

"On Rosh Hashana, all those who came to the world pass in front of Him like a flock of sheep, like walking on a small narrow road where no two can pass by at the same time...."[1]

With this saying the Talmud highlights the loneliness inherent in man's encounter with God. Human beings are, above all, individuals. They meet God privately. As such, each one is created in a different way with different talents, emotions, and potential for growth.

Still, this individuality has little value if man does not employ it to "benefit" God and his fellow man. Paradoxically, it is only in the context of a relationship that man can fully express his individuality. For if he does not encounter the "Other," he cannot be unique. Like the one wild flower a child singles out from amongst all the others to pick, so too man does not become man until his distinctiveness is highlighted.

Even so, individuality can be a great danger. The fact that each of us has a unique contribution to make to the world is a call for responsibility from which there can be no escape. One human deed, misdeed, or the absence of a deed, can decide the fate of the world. When a man acts, he reveals his thoughts and his heart. Even when his deed occurs in the context of a group each person's actions express something unique about him.

In accordance with an authoritative view in the Talmud,[2] Rosh Hashana celebrates the birth of the first human being (i.e., the first individual), while Yom Kippur reminds us of our responsibilities as

---

[1] *Rosh Hashana* 16a.
[2] *Rosh Hashana* 10b

individuals. While other creatures possess some form of individuality (for after all what is a survival instinct besides an individual will to be), their deeds do not carry moral weight and are therefore, ultimately non-distinct.

Consequently, this uniqueness of the human deed stands at the center of Rosh Hashana and Yom Kippur. The High Holidays scream out against the notion that some of man's deeds are trivial and have no moral significance. Since all his deeds take place in the presence of God, since all are the result of his free will decisions (even if in some cases they express a choice not to exercise his ability to choose), they *must*, of necessity, be significant.

The High Holidays warn us that however small our deeds may look in the eyes of man, we must always remain aware that every moment has eternal ramifications. "Time is broken eternity."[3] Consequently every moment counts. In spite of the persistent illusion, man does not have any private time; he is always with God, on God's time. He is spending God's time every second of all of his life and is therefore charged with the task of elevating all his deeds to the level of the Divine. Because he uses God's time, a man must, through his moral choices and deeds, make the passing everlasting, the common unique, and the momentary eternal.

In the minute details, man lives a life of great profundity. Detail is after all the breaking down of generalities into components subtle and refined enough to touch the Divine. Profundity is found in a pleasant tone of voice, a level of concentration, a thought of gratitude...in details, while boredom comes from living in the broad and superficial sweep.

On Rosh Hashana and Yom Kippur, we remember that we must turn every common deed into a mitzvah, making every moment a holy and dignified encounter with God. Our deeds have the power to reveal God's presence and rescue Him from oblivion. In doing the finite right, we can perceive the infinite.

---

[3] Abraham Joshua Heschel, *God in Search of Man*, Farrar, Straus, & Cudahy, NY, 1955, p. 239.

If we find ourselves pursuing new and shiny material objects, thinking that through them we might bring meaning and joy into our lives, we only need to look around us and see the depression and *inui* (suffering) from which the western world suffers. The race to grasp the fleeting excitement of new possessions leads to the trivialization of human life. We must see our possessions not as pleasure producers, but as tools with which to do *mitzvot*. Even our mundane physical objects can have great meaning in the context of a process of constant spiritual growth.

The Torah teaches us that God is concerned with the "trivialities" and "common deeds" of man. It is man's task to remember this always, and to elevate his deeds from the shallow and meaningless to the profound and eternal. This is the essence of Rosh Hashana and Yom Kippur.

34

Bereishit: Afterthoughts About Simchat Torah – The Impossible Reading

Since Simchat Torah is the day on which we celebrate the Torah, its divinity and its greatness, it is quite perplexing that there is no special mitzvah commanding the Jewish people to study Torah more deeply or for longer stretches on this festival than on any other day. In fact, if we really think about the order of the day, it turns out that very little studying can actually be done, since much of the day is occupied with dancing and singing. Even the reading of the Torah in synagogue is relatively minimal. The chazzan only recites the Torah's concluding words, which inform us about Moshe's blessings and his subsequent death; and then he reads a few opening verses from *Bereishit* that describe God's creation of the universe.

Even more remarkable is the unavailability of the text. While dancing with the Torah scrolls, they are kept carefully covered. Not once do the revelers ever undress the scrolls to show the writing on the parchment. Seemingly, we are not allowed to see the very thing we celebrate!

This leads us to wonder why it is that when we actually read from the text on all the holidays and on Shabbat, and on Mondays and Thursdays as well, we immediately cover the text as soon as the *ba'al koreh* finishes reading each section. *There seems to be a conspiracy to keep the text hidden!*

This strange phenomenon also manifests in the fact that once a page is read it immediately gets rolled up and swallowed into the scroll, to allow the next one, which was hidden, to be revealed for a short while before it too quickly disappears the moment the chazzan reaches the end of the column.

What is the meaning behind all this?

We would like to suggest that on Simchat Torah, we must once more be reminded of the Torah's exalted holiness. Even though we may understand it on some level, its true depths are inaccessible and even unapproachable.

Because the Torah seems to be within reach, we need a stern warning to remind us as we start the cycle of Torah readings anew, that we are undertaking the "impossible." There is no way to fully fathom this text. All that we can do is mine its outer layers, but never do we access the inner core of *"das ding an sich"* (the thing itself), to use Kant's expression. The Torah remains a closed book. Too much gazing at the actual Torah will leave the reader paralyzed (e.g., as he tries to contemplate the meanings of the crowns on letters or the unusual spacing between the words). Only in a secondary form, in a normal printed book *(chumash),* and with the help and guidance of the commentaries can one approach the text. Only through these commentaries does the text descend to the level of mortal man. Only when the fire of Torah is partially cooled and made "user-friendly" is there a slight chance that one may connect to some of its contents.

This is also the reason why Jews start reading the Torah but never finish. At the end of the year and especially on the day of Simchat Torah, even the greatest Torah scholars once more conclude that they need to read it again, since they only began to scratch the surface through all their previous efforts.[1]

So too, this explains why, unlike the week of Succoth during which we circle around a Sefer Torah that is placed on the *Bimah* or *Tevah* (the desk from which the Torah is read in the synagogue), on Simchat Torah we dance with the Torah scrolls so that both we and they circle around an *empty Bima/Tevah.* This time it is not the Torah as such that

---

[1] See Chapter 39, "Simchat Torah – the Endless Beginning."

stands at the center of our lives, but God, the Great Invisible, the mystery shrouded within the Torah, Who we try to encircle.[2]

Those who see the Torah as a literary work that can be studied like Shakespeare's Hamlet, a chapter out of man's great cultural heritage or as a remnant from early history of the Jews, should take this lesson to heart. The moment one disconnects the Torah from God, its source, the text loses its spirituality and slowly but surely dies, like a human left without oxygen. While studying, even only its outer layers, the student needs to be constantly reminded that this text is divine and can therefore only be approached in a state of awe and holiness. Though its words seem plain and its idiom translucent, unnoticed meanings and undreamed-of intimations are hidden beneath its apparent simplicity. The student must strain to *hear* the voice of God behind the text. It is, as Abraham Joshua Heschel once wrote, *holiness in words.*[3]

Like a centrifuge that spins around and pulls everything into its center, so too we must allow the Torah to draw us deeper and deeper into its core, for there we will find God. Only when we know that God is the Author behind these words, can we hope to (even partially) understand it.

---

[2] See *Man of Faith in the Modern World: Reflections of the Rav 2*, adapted from the lectures of Rabbi Yosef B. Soloveitchik, by Avraham R. Besdin. Ktav, NJ, 1989, Chapter 16.

[3] Abraham Joshua Heschel: *God in Search of Man*, p. 244.

35

Simchat Torah: The Endless Beginning

Jewish learning is a process of constant beginning without any end in sight. At the end of Succoth, Jews all over the world complete the reading of Torah in their synagogues, and just as soon as they reach the final word, they immediately start all over again from the beginning. This most remarkable tradition occurs on Simchat Torah. Instead of resting on our laurels, satisfied at reaching the finish line, the Jewish people annually conclude that they really did not read the Torah deeply enough, and that they must therefore go through the text again. Taking into account that this re-reading has already gone on for thousands of years, and that there are no indications it will end any time in the near future (as there are always deeper levels of insight and wisdom to be gleaned from even the most subtle nuances in the Torah), one wonders if the Jews will ever complete their reading of the Torah.

Of course, the answer is that they won't. When it comes to learning Torah, even the greatest scholars remain perpetual beginners. The text may have a beginning, but it has no end. Its words are rooted in the world of eternity. Consequently one must embark without any hope of finishing. Layers of meaning will constantly emerge. New colors appear, and as the student grows, greater revelations manifest.

But it is not only the study of the Torah scroll that never ends. The same is true for all sacred Jewish texts. When a person completes a tractate of the Mishna or Talmud, Jews gather for a festive celebration. At this party, they read a passage in which they declare their desire to start all over again. This prayer, called the *"hadran alakh"* reads: "May we return to you, tractate so and so," because we know we have not even started to understand you. The celebration is therefore not so much about finishing the tractate, but about declaring the intention to study it again from a much deeper vantage point! Getting to the end is a reason to give thanks, but the potential for growth that comes with the chance to see the same material for a second time warrants a festive meal and a proper celebration.

This stands in sharp contrast with modern, secular intellectual goals. Often, university students around the world seem far more concerned with acing tests than with acquiring wisdom or developing real expertise in any area. This attitude reveals a preoccupation with completion and so-called "success" for their own sakes.

Judaism abhors this culture of finishing without growing. In a Jewish world-view, completing a text is only valuable if it places the student in a position to begin again on a higher level. Another encounter is always necessary, because on the first time through one barely scratches the surface.

True, many secular texts are not open to such an approach. Some texts reveal the entirety of their wisdom, such that after one reading they turn stale. But if a Torah scholar ever entertains the idea that he has finished, he has not understood anything. Such a person is not even at the beginning, because in Torah, the starting line is the knowledge that there is no end.

36

Megillat Esther: The Story of Human Importance

Except for those leaders, thinkers and scientists who make a tangible contribution towards the advancement (or devastation) of mankind, it seems that the vast majority of people, numbering in the billions, do not really leave any significant impressions on the future. Were it not for their numbers, the silent masses would remain utterly invisible from history's gaze.

If we zoom out, to see the picture more objectively, however, suddenly every human being becomes staggeringly important. Let us recall the birth of Napoleon Bonaparte. Letitia Ramolino, Napoleon's mother, met her future husband, Carlos Buonaparte at the cheese market in Ajaccio. Under normal circumstances, she would not have gone there since it was her brother who normally shopped for the family. However, on that very sunny day, he decided to see some of his friends and asked his sister to take over his chores.

Letitia's brother wanted to thank his friends in person for sending him some bottles of wine that they bought on a long journey to visit their uncle in Seville, who had just come out of hospital after recovering from a bad carriage accident. The mishap in the carriage came about because one of the horses fell ill from food poisoning and lost control. This, in turn, was the result of a farmer who sold the food to a shopkeeper who then stored it in a warm place where it started to rot. And so on and so on.

This infinite causal chain made up of seemingly "trivial" events, to which no one would ascribe any significance as far as world events are concerned, ultimately led to the birth of the man who instituted the *Code Napoleon* and led an army in the battle of Waterloo!

Still, this is only a partial picture. In reality, the matter is much more complicated and infinitely more subtle. Every smile, gesture, sneeze, or silence, in fact, our very presence or absence, sets off an endless chain reaction which, like a stone tossed innocently into a pond, sends ripples into the world that in some way touch the whole of society.

Remove a single seemingly benign element from the causal web and within a few days all discussion in the country will be altered, and in a few more days the lives of billions of people around the world will be effected in some way, however miniscule. Consequently no one can ever say, "I am not important." Everyone makes a difference to the overall state of world affairs. Without each person and their choices, *everything* would be different.

But how, we should ask, can we cope with the knowledge that by one little "unimportant" act, we could unknowingly set off a causal chain leading to a terrible catastrophe? The smile we give a sick person may ultimately help him, but perhaps he will get well and subsequently cause the death of many others. Even if we decide to hole up in a secluded cabin in some rural forest and hide there until the end of our days to prevent any possibility of having an unwitting but actively negative influence on the world, how could we live with ourselves knowing that our passivity might be wreaking havoc in the web? No matter which way we turn, the veil of uncertainty will ultimately fall in front of us, and we will find ourselves in the dark. Once we act, our deeds belong to us no longer.

History offers little consolation as we see that so many times people's good intentions lead, in the end, to disaster. For example, in 1520, when Las Casas, a deeply religious priest in Cuba, discovered that the Spanish had destroyed his parish, he received permission from Cardinal Ximenes to employ a few-hundred Africans to help him rebuild it. He saved his parish and continued what he thought was a noble calling, but ultimately destroyed the lives of millions by unwittingly initiating the institution of black slave labor. This is the irony of history.

What shall a man do? And given that he can never know the ultimate outcome of his actions, to what extent is man responsible for the after-effects of his deeds?

The only reasonable conclusion is that man must take responsibility for those consequences he could clearly have seen in advance (i.e., the direct effects). He is not responsible when the impact of an action begins to branch off in unexpected ways that he could never have anticipated. Is there any reasonable sense in which we could say that Letitia's brother was *responsible* for the battle of Waterloo? In the final analysis, we must give importance to our intentions over which we have some control, and not our ultimate effects, which lie entirely beyond us.

This is one of the deeper messages of Megillat Esther. Looking carefully into the story, one sees a web of cause and effect full of the most remarkable surprises. From a rational, logical perspective, there can be no doubt that the story should have ended in the total extermination of the Jewish people. That it ends happily has little to do with any matter within the control of man.

For that reason, the sages remarked that "Esther" symbolizes the "hester panim," the hidden face of God, which means that His direct providence is only noticeable *after* the events of history unfold. What we see in the moment as an infinity of arbitrary incidents – a confusing web of coincidence – turns out to be, in hind sight, an obvious revelation of God's active role in the affairs of man.

37

War with Iraq – Only at Purim Time[1]

As the war between the USA and Iraq approaches (and is probably in full swing as readers first see this essay), one cannot escape the fact that, just like 12 years ago when the first Gulf War started, it is again the festival of Purim, and the miraculous redemption of the Jewish people from the hands of Haman hover over this conflict. This "coincidence" should not be lost on us.

In a remarkable Midrash on Mishlei, we find the following statement: "When all the other festivals will be discontinued, the festival of Purim will never be suspended."

This observation seems to fly in the face of Jewish tradition, which states categorically that the Jewish festivals mentioned in the Torah, such as Pesach, Shavuot, and Succoth will never cease to be celebrated. This idea is also mentioned by the Talmud on several occasions: "The *Mitzvot* [including the festivals] of the Torah will never be nullified, not even in the future days [i.e., the messianic age]."[2]

Rabbi Baruch Halevi Epstein, in his famous commentary *Torah Temima*, explains, in the name of his father Rabbi Yechiel Michel Halevi Epstein, this contradiction in a most original way.[3]

The miracle of Purim is very different from the miracles mentioned in the Torah. While those in the Torah were *open* miracles, such as the splitting of the Red Sea and the falling of the manna in the desert, the miracle of Purim was hidden. Unlike the miraculous events in the Torah, the Purim story does not involve violations of the laws of

---

[1] Written on the eve of the invasion of the USA army into Iraq, 2003.
[2] Jerusalem Talmud, *Megilla*.
[3] *Esther* 9:28.

nature. The Jews seem to have been saved from the hands of Haman by exceptional, but still physically possible, historical occurrences. Those who were alive at the time did not witness anything especially unusual, and the secularists surely explained the Persian Jews' salvation as the outcome of a logical chain of forces and events.

In hindsight however, we are astonished by all the accidents and incidents, each occurring in perfect sequence, and the seemingly unrelated and insignificant human acts that worked in concert to result in the complete redemption of the Jews. Recognizing the miracle from within the seemingly normal events is only possible *after* the fact.

This kind of "miracle" will never cease to exist, explains the *Torah Temima*. But the era of *open* miracles, like splitting the Red Sea, has come to an end. According to this interpretation, the above mentioned Midrash does not suggest that the actual festivals mentioned in the Torah will be nullified in future days, since this would contradict the Jewish faith,[4] but rather that the original reasons *why* they are celebrated (i.e., the open miracles) have ceased to be a feature of our experience.

One should therefore read the Midrash as follows: Open miracles which are celebrated on festivals mentioned in the Torah no longer occur, but the kind of miracles we celebrate on Purim will never be suspended. In other words: While all the other Torah festivals will still be celebrated as great *historical* events that continue to have meaning for us now, Purim, although rooted in a historical event of many years ago, will not commemorate an event in the past as much as it will function as a reminder that God's hand is still very much an active, though hidden, part of our lives. In truth, the Megilla never finished!

Rabbi Yitzchak Hutner *z"l* in his celebrated work *Pachad Yitzchak*, uses this idea to explain a highly unusual Halachic stipulation related to Purim. As is well known, on all Torah festivals, the congregation sings "Hallel," the well-known classical compilation of Psalms. These Psalms praise God for all the great miracles He performed for Israel in biblical

---

[4] See for example, Rambam's *Ikkarim*, Principle 9.

times. Why, asks the Talmud, do we not sing Hallel on Purim? Could there be a better reason to sing these Psalms than to commemorate the day on which a great miracle took place that saved Israel from the hands of Haman? The Talmud answers that *Keriyata Zu Hi Hillula* – the reading of the Megilla of Esther *is* Hallel.

In other words, by reading the story of Esther, one actually fulfills the obligation to sing Hallel because telling this story is *itself* the ultimate praise of God for saving the Jews. One of the most celebrated talmudic commentators, Rabbi Menachem Meiri, speculates about whether one should say Hallel on Purim if for some reason he was unable to read or hear the Megilla. In such a case, according to his opinion, one should indeed sing Hallel, since one has a religious obligation to express thanks to God for the miracle He performed on our behalf. Rabbi Hutner, however, turns our attention to the interesting fact that no other authority agrees with Rabbi Meiri's opinion. To the contrary, they hold that if one cannot read or hear the Megilla, he should nevertheless refrain from singing Hallel.

Rabbi Hutner explains this ruling in a most remarkable way. We sing Hallel, he writes, to praise God for *open* miracles. The verses of Hallel do not speak about *hidden* miracles. Hidden miracles should be praised in a more subtle and *hidden way* so as to remind the worshipper, both in content and form, that God does in fact run our world through marvels of this sort. Therefore it is most appropriate on Purim to read the Megilla of Esther instead of Hallel.

Megillat Esther is the story of a hidden miracle, and by reading it in front of a congregation, God receives praise implicitly. We should remind ourselves that God does not need our praises. Man needs *to* praise, as an essential part of his program of spiritual development. *How* he praises is also important. Man must praise God in such a way that he comes to understand the miracles that were done for him. Consequently, it is necessary to give praise in a manner that corresponds to the actual miracle (e.g., in an open or hidden way depending on the holiday).

Singing Hallel in place of reading the Megilla would therefore miss the point.

Without claiming to be the recipients of any Divine revelations, we dare to suggest that the war with Iraq will reflect the theme of Purim. Although it is impossible to know what will happen, it will eventually become clear that, like in the first Gulf war, Israel will experience some form of hidden miracle. Only in the years to come, when the governments involved release all the political and military information, will we realize that God worked a miracle for us. Because of the war's proximity to Purim, Jews around the world will read the Megilla and remember their Father in heaven, and will someday realize that the bizarre and exceptional circumstances under which Israel survives proves that the Purim story has only just begun.

38

The Mystery of the Karpas

While the Haggada relates the story of how God miraculously freed the Israelites, after 210 years of slavery in Egypt, there is total silence concerning the question of how our forefathers got themselves *into* this state of bondage in the first place. True, the Torah discusses this in great detail, and the festival of Pesach is meant to be a celebration of freedom rather than a painful review of historical errors, but still, it seems uncharacteristic of the Jewish tradition to completely ignore the lessons learned from slavery when recounting the Exodus in the Haggada.

With this question in mind, we notice that one of the most mysterious rituals on the Seder night involves eating of the karpas, a kind of vegetable, which we dip in salt water at the very beginning of the evening's festivities. This ritual, we are told, is designed to inspire our children (and ourselves) to ask questions. After reciting kiddush we expect to wash our hands and sit down to a proper meal like on Shabbat and on the other festivals. Instead we receive a small piece of vegetable, dip it into salty water, and remain hungry for a good part of the evening. No doubt this should make all of us ask, "why?"

Without denying the importance of this explanation for the ritual of karpas, we still need to understand why our sages decided to specifically use karpas and not some other kind of food. What is the special significance of karpas that makes it most fitting to be the catalyst for questioning during the Seder?

Rabbi Shlomo Kluger (1785–1869) in his *Yeriot Shlomo*, a commentary on the Haggada,[1] gives us a clue.[2] The word "karpas" is

---

[1] See Siddur Rabbi Yakov Emden.
[2] Rabbi Shlomo Kluger was the author of 375 books (the numerical

etymologically difficult to place, but has two distinct meanings. One relates to a vegetable. In that case its translation is celery or parsley, and this seems to be the most simple meaning in the Haggada, since we are told to partake of such a vegetable. The other understanding of karpas, however, is that it is a piece of cotton or fine linen, which brings to mind a comment Rashi makes on the brothers' hatred towards Yosef.[3] As we know, this hatred was fueled generally by their father Yakov's favoritism, but was specifically ignited when Yakov gave Yosef a special *"ketonet pasim"* – a multi-colored garment. Rashi states that the word *"pasim"* (many-colored) is an expression of *"karpas* and *techelet,"* which he translates as green and light-blue wool or linen. This statement reveals to us a secret behind the ritual of karpas on Seder night.

After Yosef received this special garment from his father, the brothers sold him as a slave to the Egyptians. This in turn led to the beginning of the exile and the enslavement of the entire Jewish people in Egypt. We see then, that the Jews' dire straits before the Exodus was indirectly caused by Yakov's gift – a garment of "karpas and techeleth" – to Yosef.

It seems that when the sages drew up the blueprint for the Passover Haggada, they wanted to draw attention to the fact that brotherly hatred caused the Jews to end up in Egypt. Realizing that this infamous garment was made of "karpas," they decided to institute a ritual involving the vegetable of the same name. On a deeper level, we recall that the brothers dipped the "karpas garment" into an animal's blood to convince their father Yakov that a wild beast killed Yosef. Thus we find a further allusion to Yosef's multi-colored garment in the custom to dip the karpas in salt water (symbolizing both blood and tears).

Still, one may wonder why the sages kept this message shrouded in obscurity. Why not mention the origins of exile explicitly in the text of

---

equivalent of his name Shlomo) and one of the most distinguished Halachic authorities of his day.

[3] *Bereishit* 37:3.

the Haggada? Why not actually place a piece of multi-colored fabric on the Seder table? If what we are saying is true, the author of the Haggada deliberately concealed this information, but then led us, via the mystery of karpas, to ask the question that would bring us to uncover the meaning behind this mysterious ritual.

This process of hide-and-seek touches the very core of the Jewish interpretation of the Exodus. From a Jewish perspective, the story of our freedom from slavery primarily serves to emphasize Divine providence in the world. God's miraculous intervention on behalf of the millions of Jews who were stranded and enslaved in Egypt had to become the *modus classicus* of all Jewish history, and in fact, of world history as well. Everything that happens is ultimately in God's hands. Conveying this message is the categorical goal of retelling the Pesach story each year. Of course, Jewish tradition constantly emphasizes that man must take responsibility for the consequences of his deeds, but the holiday of Pesach, and the meaning of the Seder operate at a deeper level of reality. On Pesach, we celebrate the revelation and triumph of God as history's active guiding force.

This interplay between Divine intervention and human action is one of the great philosophical problems with which all religious thinkers must grapple. To what extent does man deserve credit or blame for what happens here, and to what extent is God responsible? The story of the Exodus also raises many other, equally difficult theological and philosophical issues. For example, how can we ever know which cause brought about a specific effect? And when can we identify an event as a cause, and not as the outcome of something prior? Speaking in terms of the Egyptian enslavement, can we really claim that the brothers' hatred for Yosef *caused* the Jews to become Pharaoh's slaves? The Torah tells us that God promised Avraham that his descendents would be enslaved in a land that was not their own.[4] The Egyptian experience was a *sine qua non* for the Jews, a crucible in which to become worthy to receive the Torah.

---

[4] *Bereishit* 15:13.

They needed this challenge to grow as a spiritual people who could fulfill God's mission of becoming a "light unto the nations." It seems then that whether or not the brothers sold Yosef, the Jews were destined to end up in slavery somehow. To what extent then were the brothers *really* responsible for this exile? To what extent did they exercise freedom of will when they decided to sell their brother?

Perhaps because of these questions, the authors of the Haggada were not prepared to openly point fingers at the brothers. Instead the sages alluded to the fact that somewhere on the causal road to Egypt the "karpas garment" dipped in blood played a role. To what extent we may never know.

That the karpas is eaten at the very beginning of the Seder tells us straightaway that the story of what really caused the exile in Egypt will forever stay mysterious. It will indeed provoke many questions, and however brilliant the answers, we will always be left with the knowledge that on a higher plain, and beyond human understanding, only God truly understands. This is the all-encompassing, underlying message of the Haggada.

On a moral level, though, we may derive a clear message from the karpas. In some sense, hatred between brothers sent us into exile. How revealing that it was the love between two brothers, Moshe and Aaron, living in harmony, that brought about the redemption.[5]

---

[5] An important observation concerning the seder night: Since it is incorrect to teach children to steal even for fun, we suggest that the father or leader of the seder – as opposed to the children, as some practice – hide the afikoman and let them discover it to earn a reward. To make the impression on our children that the Jewish Tradition condones stealing as part of a religious ceremony is unacceptable. The reason for this prevailing custom seems to be based on a mistranslation and was never, in any way, part of the Sephardi Pesach experience.

39

Sefirat Haomer: A Day Too Late?

The biblical commandment to count 49 days between Pesach and Shavuot, encourages man to use this sacred time to take account of himself and for introspection.[1] The Exodus from Egypt marked the beginning of our forefathers' encounter with liberty, which culminated with the giving of the Torah, the law of moral freedom, at Mount Sinai. Through counting these days, we seek to engrave this sublime experience into our personalities, and thus inspire a constant elevation of our very being.

It is a major tragedy when Jews start to believe that our festivals are merely times to remember what happened thousands of years ago. We must realize that the goal of a Jewish holiday is not just to perform, but above all, to transform. Nothing is more dangerous for man than spiritual stagnation. And so God commands us to count the 49 days of the Omer. To prepare ourselves for the celebration of Shavuot, of the giving of the Torah, we try to ascend a ladder of 49 spiritual steps. Forty-nine steps in 49 days, each one adding another dimension to our souls.

The commentators express great surprise at the fact that this process of counting of the Omer starts on the *second* day of Pesach and not on the first. If the purpose of the counting is indeed to re-enact the whole historical period between Pesach and Shavuot, why not start on the day of the Exodus, the first day of the Jewish people's journey to moral freedom?

Carefully examining the events that took place on the day of the Exodus (the first day of Pesach) we notice a strange phenomenon. *Passivity.* The Jews take no action whatsoever and no initiative. They were

---

[1] *Vayikra* 23:15.

told to stay inside their homes, and simply wait for Moshe to give the sign to start leaving Egypt. There are no planned confrontations with the Egyptians, no inspirational speeches or songs, no demonstrations...just silence, absolute quiet and a spirit of waiting – still and inert. Moshe calls on them to move, and the Jewish people humbly leave Egypt after the Egyptians willingly hand over their gold and silver vessels.

God alone acted on the first day, without any human initiative or participation. God took the Jewish people out. *He* led the way. The initial stages of the Exodus were clearly exhibited. There could be no misunderstanding later about who calls the shots in the relationship between God and the Jews. The Exodus was about witnessing God's unfathomable strength and absolute sovereignty. Man must merely follow Him, like a slave follows his master.

But once the Jews cross Egypt's border, we see a radical change. After only a brief time on the road, the Israelites learn that Pharaoh and his army of chariots are approaching. The Torah reports that Pharaoh wants his slave labor force back home, and is willing to use whatever means necessary to accomplish this goal. Why, the Israelites must have wondered, doesn't God just keep Pharaoh in his palace? Only a few days prior, God ensured that Pharaoh would not even attempt to stop them from leaving!

As Pharaoh's army draws closer, the Jewish people despair. They even ask Moshe why God led them out into the desert to die.[2] It all looked so great on that first day of the Exodus! God took care of everything. So why not continue to offer such impervious protection and keep the Jews in this most comfortable situation?

Indeed, on the second day, God stopped pulling all the strings. It is as if God decided to move quietly into the background in order to force man to play a more active role in the drama. Only after they call out to Him with fervent prayers, is He then willing to step in and protect the Jews from their attackers. At the very last moment, as the Jews wade into

---

[2] *Shemot* 14:11.

the water up to their nostrils, God miraculously splits the Sea of Reeds to give them safe passage to the other side. Could God not have split the sea a little earlier to save the Jews unnecessary anguish?! Why did God put an end to the nearly messianic conditions that prevailed on that first day of the Exodus?

The point is clear: There comes a time when man must take responsibility for his spiritual growth. God did not create man and bestow nearly unlimited talents and capabilities on him for him to sit on the couch and passively rely on God to make things go the right way. God put man into the world to take moral action, to grow spiritually, and to elevate himself through hardship and struggle. The desert functioned as a classroom in which our people learned its first lessons in how to become a light to the nations and set a moral example. This is the Jewish condition, and the purpose of every Jew's life.

But why did He first let the Israelites experience a day that resembled paradise only to plunge them the next day into the depths of worry and insecurity? Because without the knowledge (via experience) that God has total power, their moral obligations would stand on quicksand. Why be moral when there is no unshakable foundation on which this morality depends? Man first has to learn that there is an existential purpose to his inner struggle to be moral, not just a utilitarian one. He first has to be convinced that there is much more to life than meets the eye – that life has a Divinely mandated purpose. First it has to become clear that God, and only God, is the ultimate source of everything. At this initial stage of development, man must merely stand in awe, overwhelmed by the grandeur of God's infinite power. Before he is able to express his own strength, to take action and become responsible for the perfection of God's world, man must first be humbled by his utter lack of power.

The struggle for moral liberty – the quest to become elevated, spiritual beings – only started the day *after* the Exodus from Egypt. The first day was a given. It was a day of God and not of man. It was a day of passivity and complete surrender. Only on the second day did the Jewish people's spiritual labor begin. In order to properly re-live the experience of the Exodus, we first have to recognize God's power, and that is what we celebrate on the first day of Pesach and focus upon in our Haggada. After we spend a day contemplating God's omnipotence until we find ourselves totally overwhelmed, then we may begin to take moral action, on the second day of Pesach.

Thus, the counting of the Omer can only start on the second day. The first day is an essential *prerequisite* to the growth process that culminates on Shavuot.

40

To Be a Matza

The Talmud[1] poses the question: Why it is forbidden to eat or posses chametz (leaven), such as bread, on Pesach? What is there in the nature of leaven that it should be forbidden on Pesach? And from the other side, what is so special about matza that makes it the most desirable food to eat on Pesach?

Rather than give a straight answer, the Talmud responds by asking still another question. Why do people sin? Understanding that human beings will continue to transgress, the Talmud analyzes one of paradoxical situations inherent to the human condition. Man desires to do good, yet he constantly struggles with his evil inclination. Realizing that the evil inclination is extremely difficult to overcome, the Talmud suggests that human beings, and especially Jews, should make the following declaration whenever they try to obey the laws of the Torah but fail to do so:

"Lord of the Universe. It is well known to You that it is our desire to do Your will. What prevents us? The yeast in the dough."

The expression, "the yeast in the dough" comes up frequently in the Talmud as a description of man's evil impulse, the reason why man does not always live up to his most treasured values nor abide by his own standards of behavior.

We now understand the seemingly circuitous answer the Talmud provides to the original question concerning the reason why it is forbidden to possess or consume leaven on Pesach. Leaven is what we get after the yeast in the dough causes it to rise. In other words, leaven is

---

[1] *Berachot* 17a.

forbidden on Pesach because it symbolizes the evil inclination – the root cause of all human transgressions!

This however begs the question. Why is the evil inclination symbolized by leaven? What does leaven do wrong that it should be used as the symbol for the evil urge in man? A closer look reveals a most fascinating idea.

Bread, chametz, is blown-up matza. What after all, is the essential difference between the two? They are made from exactly the same ingredients – flour and water – and baked in the oven. It is only the speed of preparation that makes matzah flat and hard, while bread soft and fluffy. If we bake the dough quickly, we get matza. However if the dough is left for a while, it will rise and become bread.

Practically then, the real difference between the two is *hot air* – an ingredient devoid of substance!

And it is *this* element that makes bread look so powerful and enticing in comparison to matza. It rises, becoming haughty, giving the impression that it consists of a great amount of substance while in reality it is just a cracker that is full of hot air. The matza however is humble and true to itself; there is no attempt to appear as anything more than it is – plain dough.

Bread then, is haughty matza. Thus, it symbolizes the evil inclination since it is the attitude of arrogance, blowing oneself up beyond who one truly is, which more than any other bad character trait, leads man to go astray. If a human being would just be humble, to recognize his place vis-a-vis God, then he would never contemplate transgressing His will. Only arrogance allows man to choose an undesirable path.

On Pesach, the day on which we commemorate and re-experience the inception of the Jewish people, Jews are once more reminded that their mission to become a light to the nations can only start in the spirit of true humility. Arrogance can never be the foundation of spirituality and moral integrity. Arrogance cannot truly inspire others, nor will it have a lasting effect.

Consequently, the art of spiritual growth is to become more like a matza in a world full of chametz.[2]

---

[2] Question to ponder on the Seder night: Based on the above why is Chametz not prohibited throughout the whole year? For a possible answer see Talmud *Yoma* 69b concerning the reluctance of the sages to imprison the evil inclination.

41

Pesach, and the Silence of God

The persistent absence of an explicit Divine revelation in modern times is often blamed for much of the world's secularism. Since the Renaissance, man has become increasingly skeptical of God's willingness and ability to involve Himself in the affairs of nations and men. This viewpoint in turn, has led to the collapse of religious institutions and values. As God remains hidden from us, faith becomes an ever more difficult challenge.

When the Israelites left Egypt on their way to the land of Israel, God's guiding hand was everywhere apparent. The ten plagues, the splitting of the Red Sea, and the many other spectacular open miracles showcased God's existence and power in their full glory. Consequently, modern man generally looks upon the years of wandering in the desert as an era of amazing religious clarity. Anyone living under such miraculous conditions, we surmise, would have no choice but to be a deeply holy person.

Rashi, in his commentary on the Torah, shatters this illusion: "As the result of the sin of the spies in which they spoke evil about the land of Israel, God did not speak with Moshe for 38 years."[1]

This is a most remarkable and far-reaching observation. For the vast majority of the time (38 out of 40 years!) that the Israelites traveled through the desert, God remained silent. God did not speak to them, and so the Israelites had to grapple with the question of God's involvement in their lives in a way not dissimilar to modern man. We may want to refute this view by pointing out that the manna continued to fall, and many other miracles were part of their daily lives. Nevertheless, it seems from the Torah that these phenomena ceased to impact the Israelites, as if they

---

[1] On *Vayikra* 1:2.

became spiritually desensitized. How else could they refer to the manna as *lechem hakelokel* – repulsive bread.[2] They saw these miracles as commonplace events, which should not really be so surprising given that most modern men manage to view their utterly wondrous world with apathy and boredom. We are reminded of Rabbi Dessler's famous observation that the laws of nature are nothing more than frequent miracles, a view which famous philosophers of science such as Karl Popper endorse from a secular perspective as well.[3] Indeed, on several occasions, in spite of the obvious and constant miracles happening all around them, the Israelites still asked whether God in fact lived among them!

Sitting at the Seder table, we may often feel that we are reading a story that has little in common with our modern lives. We lament God's silence, that we can no longer hear His spoken word. How then can we believe in His existence, and why should we listen to the instructions He gave to our ancestors thousands of years ago? We are today confronted with a *Deus Absconditus*, an absent God, and no story about His open intervention in history can really touch us. God's silence has made us deaf.

And even when we take stock of the fact that God did not speak with Moshe and the Israelites for 38 out of 40 years, we may still make the powerful point that we have not heard from God for more than two thousand years! How then can we be expected to deliberate with passion on events and experiences that are so totally foreign to us?

With a bit of thought, however, we may be forced to radically change our tunes. On a quantitative level, two thousand years is a much longer silence than the 38 Moshe's generation had to endure. But on a *qualitative* level, we must realize that the 38 years of silence for the Israelites in the wilderness was much more frightening than all the Divine

---

[2] *Bamidbar* 21:5.
[3] Rabbi Eliyahu Eliezer Dessler, *Michtav Me-Eliyahu 1;* and also Karl Popper, *The Logic of Scientific Discovery.*

silence of our last two thousand years. While we are, to a great extent, independent and able to take care of ourselves, this was not the case for our forefathers. They wandered through a desert wasteland without available food, water, or shelter, without which even the most elementary forms of life cannot survive. True, God provided these through miraculous means, but once God stopped speaking with them, they must have descended to the absolute depths of insecurity. This Godly silence must have been more dreadful than anything we can imagine. If God decided to stop providing them with food and water, they would die of thirst in a matter of days. This constant awareness must have been highly traumatic.[4]

When we realize that the story of the Exodus was mainly a story of Divine silence, and that God's word only entered the human realm on rare occasions, the story we read on the Seder night suddenly feels much more relevant. While the words of the Haggada relate the miracles, the "empty spaces" between the words tell us of how our ancestors must have wondered what happened to God's presence. "Where is God," they must have asked themselves every day of those devastatingly lonely 38 years. And so do we ask this question now. But just as they came through the wilderness with their faith in tact, so must we.

The lesson and the art is to hear God through the silence, and to recognize all the obvious miracles He works in His so-called "absence."

---

[4] The absence of God's word for these 38 years throws a radically different light on the Israelites' upheavals and complaints in the desert as mentioned in the Torah.

42

Plato and the Unwritten Haggada

As we prepare to gather around the Seder table and read the Haggada, the story of the Exodus of Egypt, it may be worthwhile to think for a moment about the art of reading.

Plato in his *Phaedrus* (275a–278a) and in the "Seventh Letter" (344c) questioned, and in fact attacked, the written word as completely inadequate. This may explain why philosophers have written so little about "writing," although we note that they have made use of it extensively!

Plato wrote much of his work in the form of dialogues. It becomes clear for anybody reading these "conversations" that his main purpose in doing so was to hide the characteristic of these "texts" as texts (although it is well known that he worked for years polishing these dialogues – Cicero maintains that Plato, at the age of eighty-one, actually died at his writing table. "Plato scribens mortuus est").[1]

What was Plato's problem with text?

Plato believed that written words eventually fall prey to evil and incompetent readers who twist and corrupt their meanings. And because of the nature of text, namely that it leaves the author's domain, authors are unable to defend or explain their real intentions. Plato was afraid that his texts would take on lives of their own, independent of his will. Even more interesting is his observation that a written text can become a *pharmakon* – a poison – with the power to heal or kill, depending on how one uses it. According to Plato, a text may be useful as a prompt, but will ultimately lead to memory loss since it makes the brain idle. Centuries

---

[1] Cicero, *About Old Age*, p. 13.

later Immanuel Kant wrote in similar terms when he said that the "script" wreaks havoc on the "body of memory."[2]

This however, at least according to Plato, means far more than just losing information or the ability over time to memorize accurately. Real knowledge was for him a matter of "intrinsic understanding," a total "presence" of oneself with what one reads, writes, or says. True knowledge, for Plato, is only that with which one totally identifies and which he unites entirely with his self. Information one has only read or learned by heart is not really "known." Knowledge must be inscribed on one's whole personality.

Without being aware of it, Plato touched on a most fundamental aspect of the Jewish Tradition. Although Jews are called the "People of the Book," they are not. They are the people of the ear. The Torah is not meant to be read but heard. We see this from the fact that originally it was not given in *written* form at all. God *spoke* the Divine word at Sinai, which primarily had to be heard, and which afterwards, out of pure necessity, unfortunately became frozen in a text. However, God's intention was always that even this written Torah would be "defrosted" throughout the generations, which is why Jewish Law is founded upon a great *Oral* Tradition.

When one reads, one uses one's eyes to see something that remains external to him. It does not become "inscribed" into the soul of the reader. Rabbi Yakov Leiner, the author of *Beth Yakov*, the son of the famous Ishbitzer Rebbe, Rabbi Mordechai Josef Leiner, and one of the keenest minds in the Chassidic tradition, writes that "seeing" discloses the external aspect of objects, while "hearing" reveals an aspect of their inner essence.[3] One must hear a text, not merely read it. This is the reason that the body of Torah consists of a bare minimum of written words combined with an overwhelming wealth of oral interpretation.

---

2 Immanuel Kant, *Antropologie in Pragmatischer Hinsicht*, Suhrkamp, STW 193, Frankfurt an Main, pp. 489–490.
3 Rabbi Yakov Leiner, *Beth Yakov, Rosh Chodesh Av*.

Does the open-endedness of the Torah make room for people to mis-read and mis-interpret it in ways that violate its very spirit? The Jewish Tradition responds to this dilemma by providing a set of rules of exegetical interpretation, which were handed down from Moshe, and which serve to both secure the integrity of the text and at the same time allow the student to use the full extent of his creativity and imagination within the context of the legitimate framework.

Even after the Oral Torah was written down in the form of the Talmud, it remained very much unwritten (as any Talmud student can testify). No other text is so abbreviated, succinct, and "understaffed" with written words, and simultaneously overflowing with meaning to the point of explosiveness. The art of Talmud can only be learned via a close teacher-student relationship and not through the written word alone, because only when the student hears his master's interpretations of the text can he "read" it properly. And by spending enough time with the rabbi and the text, the student will eventually learn to "hear" the interpretations singing through the text.

The teacher does not only give interpretations, however, but also conveys some of the inner vibrations that were once heard at the revelation at mount Sinai. This inner knowledge that the teacher himself received from his teachers, is a process that goes back all the way to the supreme moment at Sinai. In this way, the Jewish Tradition frees itself from Plato's paradox. The Talmud scholar hears new voices explaining the old text in new ways, but without deviating from its Author's intended meaning. At the same time, the student learns in time to think creatively on his own but without personal biases getting in the way of truth. As such, the text is not read, but truly heard.

Jewish law specifies that even if one finds himself alone on Seder night, he must *pronounce* the text of the Haggada out loud, and not just read it silently to himself. In such a case, one must hear oneself speaking the words. One must also interpret and explain the text to oneself in a verbal way. The head, which understands quickly, must speak to the heart in a dialogue so a person can actually feel what happened to his ancestors thousands of years ago.

Perhaps we can understand Plato's paranoia about his own writings: they are too much read and too little heard. This may, however, just be a function of the difference between human words and those authored by the Divine. Human words are too much grounded in the text. The Divine word is beyond textual limitations and henceforth can only begin to express its meaning through the act of speaking and listening, as it is the sense of hearing that brings words inside a person's mind (literally via the soundwaves), so he may perhaps feel the tingling from the vibrations that emanate from a world beyond.

When Jews on the Seder night read the text of the Haggada, they should be aware that the text merely provides a starting point. The real Haggada does not have a script. It is not a dialogue that can be read but must be said and heard aloud, and then contemplated endlessly.

43

Shavuot:
Rabbi Yochanan ben Zakai and the Portable Fatherland

In a fascinating narrative in the Talmudic tractate of *Gitin* (56b), we are told that Rabbi Yochanan ben Zakai, outstanding leader of the Jewish people during the Roman invasion of the land of Israel, was confronted with a question of life and death. Vespasian, who would soon become the Roman emperor, brought the Jews to a point of utter exhaustion after years of siege and battle. Jerusalem fell. People were dying. There was nothing to eat, and despair overtook the Jewish community. They knew the (second) Temple would be looted and destroyed at any moment. There was no way for the Jews to rid themselves of the enemy and so only one question remained: To surrender and live, or fight valiantly to the death?

Rabbi Yochanan, a "moderate," made a crucial decision that saved Judaism and sent a great message to all future generations of Jews.

His disciples smuggled him in a coffin out of the besieged city to bring him to the soon-to-become emperor, Vespasian. When asked why he came, Rabbi Yochanan responded that the Jews were willing to surrender on one condition: "Give me Yavne and its sages."

The city of Yavne was the center of Jewish learning and the seat of a most outstanding Beth Din (rabbinical court) at the time, and was thus the home of many influential sages. This seemed to be a minor request and Vespasian, seeing no harm in such a humble petition, agreed. Little did he know that this agreement would ultimately allow the Jews to outlive the Romans by thousands of years. Neither did those Jews who opposed this capitulation realize that Rabbi Yochanan's agreement with Vespasian was in fact a splendid victory for the Jewish people.

Rabbi Yochanan understood that the issue of Jewish survival does not depend on the possession of the land of Israel or maintaining a strong army, but rather on a strong sense of identity, an ideology and a deep love and understanding of the Torah. For other nations, possession of a land and political institutions are essential to their existence. But for Jews, this is not the case. Although Rabbi Yochanan did not deny the centrality of the land of Israel, he knew that it would be possible for Jews to continue to be a people without a land. To do so might be dangerous, and certainly far from the ideal. Giving up Yerushalayim would bring the Jewish people to the brink, but as long as they remained idealistic and connected to the Torah, Rabbi Yochanan knew his strategy would work in the long run.

Thus he made a most unconventional move that turned the Jewish people on its head. He created what Heinrich Heine called a "portable fatherland." This "land" was none other than the covenant with God – the Torah – and the Jewish people would carry this portable country in their hearts and minds, into lands of exile for centuries.

Rabbi Yochanan realized that the land of Israel did not make the Jews fitting to live by the Torah, but that living by the Torah makes the Jews fit to inherit the land. Not for love of the land do Jews stay Jews, but because of their ongoing love affair with God's text and words.

Still, Rabbi Yochanan knew that the text alone would not accomplish the goal of Jewish survival and continuity, but rather the vibrant *encounter* with the biblical text would keep the Jews alive in exile. Only a constant, living dialogue with the Torah can transform the Jews into an eternal people, guaranteeing Israel's capacity to overcome all of its enemies. As long as the Jews keep living the text, they will not die.

Rabbi Yochanan's gambit was revolutionary because it also required Jews throughout the generations to debate with the great sages of the past. They would argue with them as if they were alive and sitting at their feet in the great Talmudic academies, studying this text together through space and time. Landless and powerless, Jews would inhabit a mental universe whose horizons would be more vast than all the empires on the planet combined. With this in mind, Rabbi Yochanan "surrendered" to Vespasian. He knew that keeping the academy at Yavne flourishing would in time lead to an unprecedented victory – that the Jewish people would outlive the Roman empire and ultimately come back to Israel.

"Give me Yavne and its sages." By receiving this concession from Vespasian, he had not only safeguarded the Torah and its sages but above all the people of Israel. By laying the foundations of the portable land of the Jews, he in fact guaranteed their glorious future.

Still, Rabbi Yochanan ben Zakai realized that learning alone would not be enough. The Jews needed a place where they would experience the Torah being lived on a day-to-day level. Unlike the great academies of Greece, Yavne was not merely a place of theoretical study. Greek and Roman philosophy was *thought*, but not *lived*. By giving the sages of Yavne the opportunity to study and teach together in a proper *makom Torah*, Rabbi Yochanan knew they would live the truth, transforming the "ought" of Judaism into an "is." The integrity of the sages of Yavne guaranteed that Jews would never succumb to moral bankruptcy and hypocrisy like so many Greeks and others who taught ethics and law but did not live according to their so-called truths.

Yavne would prevail because the sages there would not teach philosophy, but life; not faith taught, but faith lived. As Franz Rosenzweig so aptly said: It is in the *deed* that one really hears, it is in the performance of a religious *act* that one becomes a man of faith.

Shavuot is therefore not just the celebration of the giving of the Torah at Sinai many thousands of years ago, but also the commemoration of Rabbi Yochanan's heroic "surrender." This single act, based on unbelievable foresight, turned out to be a victory that kept the Jews alive and brought them back home nearly two thousand years later. In so doing he sent a resounding message to all the inhabitants of the land of Israel in our generation: It is not the land or its army that will allow us to defeat our enemies. It is our "portable fatherland," the Torah, that protects us and ensures our survival.

44

The Destructionist Synagogues: The Ceremonial Hall, the Nostalgia Center, and the Davening Club

In his exciting book, *On Being a Jew*, Professor James Kugel warns his readers about three kinds of synagogues that have done great damage to Jewish life. He calls them the "Ceremonial Hall Synagogue," the "Nostalgia Center" and the "Davening Club."[1]

In the Ceremonial Hall, the congregation is essentially an audience. This kind of synagogue reminds one of a movie house or a theatre where people go to be entertained by a cast of players – in this case by the rabbi and the cantor. The Ceremonial Hall exists principally to solemnize major life events such as holidays, weddings, funerals, and bar and bat mitzvah celebrations. The congregants merely "attend" such occasions. They do not come in search of God or to repent or to grow in any way, but rather to listen passively to an often overly dramatic cantor or a sermon "to which they listen with the discerning attention of theater-goers marooned in an unwanted matinee."[2]

After the service is over the so-called "worshippers" exchange pleasantries and make observations about the performance that remind us of the kinds of comments made by second-rate Broadway critics: "He really had it this morning, didn't he?" or, "Much better than last year, wasn't it?" or even better, "I am glad that they got rid of that other fellow!"

Prayer is a way to turn the inferior into the important, to transform the trivial into the magnificent, to lift man from the mediocre to the supreme.

---

[1] James Kugel, *On Being a Jew*, Harper Collins, NY, 1990.
[2] Ibid.

The second variety of synagogue is the Nostalgia Center, where the rabbi is generally the youngest member. A Nostalgia Center rests in what was once a vibrant community, but the participants did not instill their children with Jewish values so that when they grew old, the synagogue turned into a place to say Kaddish, where Judaism becomes identified with the old and the deceased. Its members delight in their young rabbi's energy and passion for God because he represents what they lost a long time ago. They do not realize the reason for their lack of spiritual vitality: when they were young, they did not labor constantly to revitalize their Judaism within themselves.

Prayer is not about what "was," but about what is and will be. It is the art of setting one's inner soul to the music and light that God bestows on man anew every day.

And then there is the "davening club," the "prayer club" in which young people come together to "obdavnen" (i.e., to pray by routine, frantically mumbling words, the meaning and value of which is lost on the community as they try to get out the door as quickly as possible). Everybody in the davening club participates in the prayers, and no doubt it is the most authentic of all three places of worship. But how many people leave such a service spiritually uplifted? How many feel transformed by the experience?

"We do not step out of the world when we pray. We merely see the world in a different setting. The self is not the hub, but the spoke of the revolving wheel. In prayer we shift the center of living from self-consciousness to self-surrender. God is the center to which all forces tend. He is the source and we are the flowing of His force, the ebb and flow of His tides. Prayer takes the mind out of the narrowness of self-interest, and enables us to see the world through the lens of the holy. For when we push ourselves to the extreme opposite of ego, we can almost behold our situation from the perspective of God."[3]

---

[3] Abraham Joshua Heschel, *I Asked for Wonder*, edited by Samuel H. Dresner, Crossroad NY, 1983, p. 20.

161

45

It's Time to Go to Synagogue: The Wisdom of an *Apikores*

In my younger days, I knew a convinced and committed *apikores* (heretic). I used to meet him every Shabbat morning in synagogue where he was a frequent worshipper. He would often walk into the sanctuary, tell people that they were wasting their time coming to the morning service since "there is no God," and then he would walk to his usual place, cover himself with his *talit*, open his prayer book, and recite the prayer service with great fervor.

Intrigued by his behavior, I once asked him to explain himself. What is a committed atheist doing in a synagogue, praying as if his life depends on it? After a short pause he said, "The reason why I come to synagogue and join in the prayers is the same reason I make Kiddush at home on Friday night and eat kosher. I am a Jew, and I want to identify as a Jew. And the observance of these customs is what makes us Jews. The synagogue is where we Jews meet as Jews, and these prayers give us our *neshomeh* (Jewish soul). Without these we are lost. So I come. And I will continue to come to this synagogue 'till my last day on earth, and I will eat kosher and make Kiddush Friday night. True, there is no God, but I am a Jew!"

In these trying days for the people of Israel, I am finally able to understand the wisdom of this Jewish *apikores*. Those who carefully read Israeli newspapers, listen to the radio, and watch debates on television cannot escape the fact that many leading and highly intelligent Israelis no longer care about their Judaism. They seem to have lost their *neshomehs* They have almost completely separated themselves from the community of Israel. Unlike my friend, the heretic, who was a *Jewish apikores*, their brand of heresy is entirely secular. And that is the difference between heaven and earth.

Denying the Jewishness of the Israeli State, or distorting it so that it loses all meaning, will have disastrous consequences. To question the moral justification of the State of Israel is critical. Telling fellow Jews that we should have founded our new homeland in Uganda is destructive. Suggesting that we change "Hatikva" in order to remove its Zionist message, or that we replace the Israeli flag with a non-Jewish symbol is devastating. Trying to replace 4000 years of Jewish Tradition with 50 years of Israeli culture is a tragedy. Even putting forth such a proposal demonstrates that a person has lost his *neshomeh*.

Professors in Israeli universities have taught thousands of Israeli students a kind of nihilism, rejecting Jewish values and declaring them to be outdated antiquities of our primitive forefathers. Famous Israeli authors have declared war upon the Jewish Tradition. Zionist leaders, once heroes in the minds of secular Israelis, are now ridiculed and portrayed as villains. Left-wing Israeli historians have made it their mission to prove that Jews never lived in this country, that the Temple never stood in Jerusalem and that there is no authentic Jewish claim to the land. Pop music has replaced Zionist and Jewish melodies, and drug and alcohol abuse is coming increasingly into style among the Israeli youth.

There is no greater danger to a nation than the demoralization and destabilization that comes from convincing it that its origins have no value, that their people's traditions are meaningless, that their ideology is bankrupt, and that their claim to the land is unethical. These views are treasonous and suicidal.

While the vast majority of young Israelis still call themselves Jewish, it is abundantly clear that more and more of them no longer see this as a privilege. Those who carefully observe the society in the land of Israel cannot escape the feeling that some kind of epidemic is spreading over the country. It contaminates the nation's inhabitants with an anti-

Jewish spirit, and tries to pave the way for a Judaism-free culture to take over. This plague abrades the Jewish *neshomeh*, strangles and kills it.

The Jewish *neshomeh*, Heaven forbid, is being buried in the sacred earth of the holy land. Even if the secular Israelis perform the funeral with the dignity one accords to the ancient world and one's forefathers, they will ultimately wake up one day and realize that they destroyed the very foundation of their state, their very identity, and their future. Their cries for help in the aftermath will be of no avail, and their attempt to resurrect the Jewish *neshomeh* will be too little too late.

True, the land of Israel is blessed with many, many proud Jews who take their Judaism very seriously and embrace the country with all the love in their souls. But these are mainly found within the religious or traditional communities. Regrettably we see simultaneously a whole generation of fine, young, secular Israeli children falling victim to a poisonous desire to out-goy the goyim. While their parents still possess some kind of Jewish education, these children are rapidly falling away from their roots.

Concerning them, the handwriting is on the wall. Having been robbed by the anti-religious culture of proper and inspirational Jewish education and a warm Jewish environment, they will no longer relate to the uniqueness of their Jewish *neshomehs*. They will be left without an ideology and without love for the land. They will turn into people who despise themselves for what they are. This mentality, more than the murderous intentions of our enemies, poses the biggest threat, God forbid, to the State of Israel's survival.

Israelis should therefore, return to the synagogue and to some level of Jewish practice. That they are secular, *apikorsim*, or atheists does not worry us as much as the fact that they are losing their *neshomehs*. They should listen to my friend, the *Jewish apikores*. Israeli society must rediscover its Jewish *neshomeh* and once more discover the joy of Jewishness. The Jewish *neshomeh* is only fashioned in the synagogue and in a genuine Jewish environment where it can be kept warm and spiced with its special flavor.

Government ministers, Knesset members, Israeli professors, historians, and influential authors especially should go to synagogue, to set an example and to rediscover their Jewish *neshomehs*. The experience could be enlightening for them, bringing warmth back to their souls. Even though some of them may continue to be *apikorsim* or secularists, they will nevertheless at least develop a sense of pride about being Jewish. Above all, the people of Israel will see their leaders in synagogue and feel assured that their they are not just members of an Israeli state, but Jews. Such a development would bring great relief and a great *simcha* to millions of Jews around the world.

And when our enemies hear, they will finally understand that the Jewish spirit is not to be ridiculed and will never be crushed.

46

Finding One's *Neshomeh:*
Franz Rosenzweig and the Berliner Shtiebl

Israeli leaders, academics, and the Israeli public should find their way back to the synagogue to rediscover their *neshomehs*, but this is no doubt easier said than done.[1] Many enter and leave without sensing any spiritual significance. In fact, many who enter feel actively discouraged by the experience.

Coming to synagogue is a skill and an art. One has to arrive with a sincere urge to discover one's Jewishness, to reconnect with the Jewish people, with one's inner being, and with God. To enter the synagogue properly one must hope to transform his soul and personality.

When Franz Rosenzweig (Germany, 1886–1929) decided to leave Judaism and be baptized, he said his final farewell to the religion of his birth by attending the High Holiday services in a shtiebl, a small unconventional orthodox synagogue, in Berlin. Arguing the case for conversion he wrote: "We (Jews) are Christians in everything. We live in a Christian state, attend Christian schools, read Christian books; in short our whole culture rests entirely on Christian foundations. Therefore if a man has nothing to hold him back, he needs only a slight push...to make him accept Christianity."[2]

To his utter surprise, Rosenzweig found himself deeply inspired by the services. He underwent a religious metamorphosis and left the

---

[1] Quoted by Samuel Hugo Bergman, *Faith and Reason, Modern Jewish Thought*, Schocken Books, 1961, p. 57.
[2] Rosenzweig's most important work is *The Star of Redemption*. For a thorough critique, see Eliezer Berkovits, *Major themes in Modern Philosophies of Judaism*, Ktav, 1974, chapter 2.

small synagogue with a profound love for his Judaism. Not only did he call off his decision to become a Christian, but decided to look into the possibility of becoming a religious Jew. Consequently, he made a very intensive study of Judaism, wrote some remarkable works about his newly found faith and became one of the most important modern Jewish thinkers.

What happened to Rosenzweig during the span of a few hours in that small synagogue? What turned his whole life around and transformed him into a deeply religious Jew? How is such a metamorphosis possible, especially for a man of great intellect and education? Rosenzweig, after all, had spent years studying philosophy and contemplating Christianity. He had discussed this with many of his friends who had encouraged him to go ahead with his conversion. Still, within a few hours he decided to disregard the whole edifice on which he based his earlier decision and decided instead to commit himself on some level to Judaism!

The solution to this problem may be found in a highly significant Midrash that tells the story of a Jewish apostate named Yosef Mechita, who helped the Romans destroy the Temple.

"When the enemies (the Romans) desired to enter the Temple Mount, they said, 'Let one of them (the Jews) enter first.' They said to Yosef Mechita, 'Enter and whatever you bring out is yours.' So he went in and brought out a golden lamp. They said to him, 'It is not fitting for a common person to use this, so go in, and whatever you bring out is yours.' This time, he refused. Said Rabbi Pinchas: 'They offered him three years taxes, yet he still refused and said, "Is it not enough that I have angered my God once that I should anger Him again?"' What did they do to him? They put him into a carpenters clamp and sawed him and dismembered him. He cried: Woe to me that I angered my Creator!"[3]

Rabbi Yosef Kahaneman, the founder of the famous Ponevezh Yeshiva in B'nei Berak, once commented that this Midrash conveys the mighty influence the Temple had on human beings who stepped within

---

[3] *Midrash Rabba, Bereishit* 45:22.

its sacred walls. The moment Yosef Mechita entered the Temple he underwent a spiritual metamorphosis. He suddenly felt that he was a Jew and was deeply touched by the unique atmosphere and the energy from the symbols and vessels he saw inside. He still "managed" to take out a golden lamp, but once outside he realized he could no longer deny his Jewishness. Desecrating the Temple for a second time became an impossible feat. His newly-found *neshomeh* did not allow him to transgress. Even when the Romans offered him great amounts of money and threatened to torture him to death, he could not get himself to defile the House of God again.

In his weekly *Parasha* commentary, Rabbi Yissachar Frand suggests that this Midrash explains how Franz Rosenzweig could be transformed by his experience in the Berliner shtiebl.[4] Once he saw Jews praying sincerely, with *talitot* over their heads, and deep in concentration, his *neshomeh* awoke and his Jewishness was restored.

This, however, needs further explanation: How do a synagogue and Jewish prayers suddenly awaken a totally dormant Jewish soul? What overwhelming spiritual power rested within the Temple that caused Yosef Mechita to suddenly become conscious of his Creator? Much, we would argue, depends on the attitude we bring with us into the Temple or synagogue. After all, many enter and leave disappointed or even discouraged. Other people in history defiled the sanctuary and did not show any remorse. Most notably, Titus, the Roman, entered the Temple and engaged in debaucherous acts with two harlots in the Holy of Holies![5]

According to kabbalistic thought, the physical vessels in the Temple, such as the altar and the menorah, were tangible and symbolic reflections of the *Ein Sof*, the infinite Divine "Being," which, like a kind of fog, descended into this world. These symbols are not fully comprehensible, since their essence belongs to the metaphysical realm.

---

[4] *Parashat Toledot: Wer ist Weise?* (German).
[5] *Gitin* 56b.

They are, however, identified and recognized by the subconscious which itself has its roots in the Divine, since man was formed in the Divine image. Consequently, these vessels evoked an overwhelming perception and recognition of the higher worlds, which gave the worshiper the unique feeling of looking into his own soul. Seeing the Divine, as symbolized by the Temple vessels, allowed a person to recognize the Divine within himself, and thus to perceive his *neshomeh* clearly. This encounter would ultimately lead to the kind of spiritual awakening and metamorphosis that Yosef Mechita experienced when he entered the Temple.

Perhaps in a similar way, Franz Rosenzweig discovered his own *neshomeh* while attending High Holiday services in the shtiebl in Berlin. Once he saw the symbolic objects in the synagogue (representing the Temple), and simultaneously heard and read the High Holiday prayers, he entered subconsciously into a heavenly realm that had been all the time hovering within his soul. Those few hours of meditation revealed and revolutionized his inner being.

This is what we suggest all secular Israelis try to accomplish, to enter a small synagogue filled with dedicated and passionate worshippers, to absorb their surroundings and "let go," and thus allow themselves to feel their souls. This indeed requires great courage, but the sudden feeling of familiarity and belonging that will result from an encounter with the world of the *neshomeh* will be one of unexpected bliss. It will be a "homecoming" that will ultimately save the Jewish world from a great amount of self-inflicted suffering.

47

The Curse of Fluency

"And the Lord said: For as much as this people draw near, and with their mouth and with their lips do honor Me, but they have removed their heart far from Me and their fear of Me is like rote learning from human commands." —*Yeshaya* 29:13

In this biting critique, the prophet protests against one of the most common failures of those who pray.

The art of prayer in the Jewish Tradition presents the faithful with a paradoxical challenge. On one hand, one must carefully follow the words of the prayer book and not to deviate from them. The sages with their understanding of the spiritual universe and insight into the human soul were able to create words of prayer with the ability to elevate man and connect him to God. After they determined the best possible combination of words, the sages institutionalized them as the liturgy for prayer.

This came at great potential peril. A set script can easily be learned by rote after so much repetition. As a consequence, the deep meaning and inspirational aspects of the words can get totally lost, at which point davening just becomes a mechanical performance. Scholars have called this phenomenon *Der Fluch der Gelaeufigkeit* – the curse of fluency.

To combat this problem, the sages instructed that we pray with *kavana*, the spiritual intent and concentration we maintain while praying in an attempt to feel the music ringing within words. Without this extra effort, much of prayer becomes almost meaningless.

Maintaining the proper level of *kavana*, however, has never been an easy matter, not even for the most pious. All of us occasionally succumb to the curse of fluency, which can easily lead to other more serious problems. The worshippers may be so haughtily satisfied with their ability to say the words quickly and correctly, that they completely forget in front of Whom they stand. They no longer speak or listen to God, but listen to themselves. Their prayers become directed more at themselves than at God. At other times the worshipper does not even hear himself, since he can say the words without thinking and his mind is free to wander somewhere else altogether. In that case there is no audience at all, and the prayers go nowhere. Another not uncommon pitfall occurs when elements of competitiveness set in, whereby a worshipper tries to outdo his neighbor. This may result in a kind of game in which the real objective is to pray more loudly or even longer (or shorter) than one's fellow congregant. One no more thinks of God, but of one's neighbor. The result is Godless prayer.

Besides the need for the worshipper to use all the techniques available to him to fight and overcome these problems (e.g., via careful study of the prayers, meditation, singing, etc.), it is also the task of the chazzan to save his congregation from these potential snares. His task is to provide a living example and a *commentary* on the prayer book while leading the service. The intonation of his voice, his emotional connection with the prayer book, and his body language – even his facial expressions should instill vibrancy and meaning into the prayers and elevate his congregation to a higher levels of God-consciousness. The chazzan should be trying to foment a revolution in the souls of his fellow Jews.

So too, the Torah reading in synagogue is often diminished by this "curse of fluency." Some *"ba'alei koreh"* (those who read the Torah on behalf of the congregation) have become such experts and fluent readers that they fly through the Torah's vowel-less text with ease, at an amazing pace, without making even the slightest mistake. One gets the impression that they are coasting over smooth ice, while their minds may or may not be at all engaged with the words they are singing. Often their performances display no emotion whatsoever, other than perhaps a hint of boredom with the task at hand.

A Torah text should be read and rendered as a poem, with all the intonations and vibrations indicated in the traditional *"trop"* (the Torah's musical score as set by our Tradition). The *ba'al koreh*, like the chazzan, has to throw himself into the text completely and experience the drama as if he had never read it before. He must feel totally involved as he sits with Josef in Pharaoh's prison and travels with the Israelites through the desert on their way to Sinai. The Torah text must "hit" him, and he should walk away from it in a state of exaltation, overwhelmed by its message and the reality of its divine source. He must read with the awareness that the Creator of the universe gave us the text as a means to connect with Him. Only *then* has he actually read the Torah as it was meant to be read.

Every chazzan and *ba'al koreh* must find a way to inspire himself and his congregation so as not to get trapped by this curse of fluency. With some effort, each prayer service and each Torah reading should, and can, be an exhilarating and unforgettable experience.

48

Prayers for the Wicked[1]

We live in an age of war and constant concern for our own security. Nevertheless, committed Jews have a special obligation to push their hearts and minds into regions of moral space where others are unable or unwilling to venture. The modern Jew must take time to contemplate the enormous cost, in terms of loss of life, of the wars around the world (such as in Iraq). In battles raging right now, human beings on both sides of the conflict are dying horribly violent deaths.

Firstly, we must consider the remnants of the small Jewish community in Baghdad who find themselves embroiled in the hostilities, and who will likely incur losses before the fighting ends. Then there are the many innocent Iraqis who opposed Saddam and who would just like to live in peace. This of course includes many women and children. And finally, we must also think about the many American and British soldiers. All will lose, and some will die.

In light of the above, we are well advised to listen to the words of the great Neziv, Rabbi Naftali Zvi Yehudah Berlin *z"l*, the last Rosh Hayeshiva of Yeshivath Volozhin, the most prestigious Talmudic Institution in Eastern Europe before World War II. In his magnum opus *Ha'emek Davar*, Neziv asks why the sages referred to the book of *Bereishit* as the "Sefer HaYashar," the book of those who are straight and upright. His response is most telling.[2]

"The reason for this is on account of the great praise which the Torah bestows on the patriarchs. They were not only righteous and pious in ways far beyond the norm, but also uncompromising when it came to

---

[1] Written at the outbreak of the Iraqi war in 1991.
[2] See his introduction to *Bereishit*.

straightforwardness and honesty. The patriarchs dealt pleasantly with the most heinous idol worshippers of their days and were concerned with their welfare. This we can see in the case of Abraham who prayed for the wellbeing of the wicked people of Sodom.[3] Even though he despised their deeds, he still sought their wellbeing, in the same way that a man can hate the wicked deeds of his beloved children. Therefore, Abraham was called the "Father of the Nations." And so too, we see this idea reflected in the life of Yitzchak, who appeased the wicked shepherds who stole his water wells, and who moved his camp rather than force a fight.[4] Yakov also demonstrated this character trait, for example, when he dealt with his wicked father-in-law, Laban, with great mercy, even though the latter constantly deceived him and sought to destroy his family."[5]

While relatively few *mitzvot* are found in *Bereishit*, the outstanding example set by the patriarchs stands as a constant reminder of what God demands from His chosen people: constant concern *even* for the wicked. This does not imply that one cannot fight the wicked when they become a threat. Failure to defend oneself against violent enemies constitutes a clear transgression of Torah law. Even Avraham waged war against and killed several wicked kings,[6] but when the wicked did not pose any real threat to him or his family, he demonstrated an unusual sensitivity for even the most depraved people in his generation.

While this war in Iraq might be necessary in order to remove one of the most dangerous men of our times from power and to establish greater peace and security in the Middle East region, we should use this occasion as an opportunity to emulate Avraham Avinu. We should pray not only for the soldiers on our side, but also for those many innocent people in Iraq who are losing their lives together with the troops. As taught by Avraham, we should pray on behalf of wicked people, as long

---

[3] *Bereishit* 18.
[4] *Bereishit* 18.
[5] *Bereishit* 29–30.
[6] *Bereishit* 14.

as they pose no direct threat to us, that they will live to repent.[7] After all, one of the great lessons of the Jewish heritage is that every human being carries a spark of God in his soul that may one day ignite and inspire him to become righteous. Human beings always carry the potential to reverse the flow of inertia and surprise, as our free will allows us to break out of the cage of deterministic forces. Each person has the capacity to change and to repent, and so we Jews should pray that they will.

---

[7] It may seem inconsistent that we ask God to destroy the wicked three times each day in the eighteen benedictions (i.e., the *Shemoneh Esrei* or *Amida*). However, this prayer refers to wicked people who pose a direct threat and who cannot be stopped in any other way. For a full elucidation of this prayer see *Netiv Bina 2* by Rabbi B.S. Yakovson, chapter 9 with a special reference to the observations of Rabbi Avraham Yitzchak Kook. See also the observations made by the famous Rabbi Yakov Emden (1697–1776) in his *Siddur Beth El*, pp. 133–134 where he declares that the wickedness referred to in this prayer is extremely rare among the nations, and that we recite the prayer as a preventative measure, so that such evil will not raise its head again!

49

Ilan Ramon, *z"l*

The first human astronaut to leave our atmosphere for outer space was Phileas Fogg. He was launched there in the imagination of Jules Verne, famed author of *20,000 Leagues Under the Sea* and *Journey to the Center of the Earth*. The launch took place in the year 1873 and became known worldwide through Verne's masterpiece *Around the World in 80 Days*.

At the time, few people believed that such a journey would ever be possible. Indeed, even, Verne was nervous as to whether his hero would indeed succeed in his travels within the set time limit. In the end, Fogg's money, courage, and English pluck, as well as the 24-hour time difference between the hemispheres, made it possible for him to return on time, although he cut it close.

Those involved in space exploration today do not think any more in terms of days, hours, minutes, or even seconds. Ilan Ramon *z"l* and his fellow astronauts journeyed more than six million miles in just 16 days,[1] and though he was still in space, Ilan was only 16 minutes away from his earthly destination when he tragically departed from this world.

Space travel has introduced us to completely different dimensions of our existence. These new realms are not coming into consciousness as the result of a slow and steady development, nor are they emerging from what in retrospect seem to be obvious breakthroughs. At an ever increasing rate, we are starting to see revolutionary changes appearing in our world that no one would have even considered contemplating a few years ago. Suddenly, we realize that we are walking through the door of a new epoch before we even thought to ring the bell. "Proportionally" and in accordance with the normal rates of scientific development, it should

---

[1] *Jerusalem Post*, February 5, 2002.

have been impossible for people to fly a distance of several million miles in 16 days only a couple hundred years after the Wright Brothers's first flight at Kitty Hawk. Alvin Toffler in his remarkable book *Future Shock* tells us that there is widespread agreement among historians, archeologists, scientists, sociologists, economists, and psychologists that social and scientific processes are *speeding up* – far beyond our understanding or wildest dreams.[2]

The Kabbala tells us that a great acceleration will take place in the days prior to the messianic age. Just like the members of a Jewish home start hurrying on Friday afternoon to ensure that everything will be ready for Shabbat, so too the world starts to rush when the messianic age, the ultimate Sabbath, begins to approach. This idea is based on the verse: "I, God will accelerate *it* in its time."[3] The *"it"* here, is understood to be an allusion to the messianic era.

In times of great instability, the possibility of the ultimate Sabbath becomes so overwhelming and appealing that it begins to force its way forward. But with great speed comes the risk of accidents. Trying to do too much in too little time, while perhaps necessary, increases the probability for error, as this may entail a lack of sufficient preparation.

The greatest problem, however, is that the overwhelming speed of our development relies heavily on technology that leaves very little for man himself to do. Most of the journey into space is pre-set by computers and beyond human control. Man, the original architect of the space shuttle and its numerous support systems (oxygen, insulation, fuel, electrics, etc.) slowly but surely subordinates himself to his own inventions and then loses his identity as man. Eventually, he turns himself into an instrument that takes care of his machines.

In an interview, Major Gagarin, the first Russian astronaut, was asked what was the most important event in his life. He promptly answered, "The twelfth of April when I became a member of the

---

[2] Alvin Toffler, *Future Shock*, Bodily Head, London, 1970.
[3] Isaiah 60:22, Zohar 1:116b–117a.

communist party." This too was automatic. He had become part of a system that stripped him of his humanity. When a famous Dutch author met a man who spoke 12 languages, he paused for a moment and asked, "But do you also have something to say in these languages?" This is of the essence. After all, what is the purpose of knowing many languages when one has nothing to communicate? Just learning languages to be useful as a translator, but without thinking enough to say something interesting or inspirational in any language also hints at this trend of automatization.

Sending people into space to consequently reduce them into unthinking robots is an embarrassment for all of mankind. The glorification of such a powerful and sophisticated space shuttle and the sad simplicity of such a man is too much to bear. When a man with the potential of Gagarin can truly see his official entry into the club of "yes-men" as the climax of his life, then we are at a most dangerous historical crossroads. He may have left the Earth's atmosphere and traveled through space, but he never even began to expand his mind.

It was the great merit of Ilan Ramon *z"l* that he lifted himself, and all of us with him, beyond the slightest possibility of becoming automatized. Not only did he stay beautifully human in space, but he elevated his humanity. He taught the Jewish people that one should not become an indistinguishable number among the many. He refused to go along with the "yes-men" who are obsessed with the gentile world, and who therefore call for the total secularization of Israel.

While in space Ilan emphasized the unique greatness of being Jewish, making sure to take a Sefer Torah, a Kiddush cup, and other religious items with him on his journey. His view was broader than many of his assimilated fellow Jews, and as such he made a *kiddush Hashem,* and no doubt left outer space for an even higher destination.

May his memory be blessed.

50

After Modern Orthodoxy, Then What?[1]

Introducing Chief Rabbi Professor Jonathan Sacks

As we know everything is anticipated in the Torah. So where do we find the source for preliminary remarks to introduce a Chief?

We find the Torah's guidance for such an occasion in *Sefer Bereishit, Parashat Lech Lecha*. There God gives a major lecture to inform Avraham about the impending birth of his son Yitzchak and the future of the Jewish people.

This speech was introduced by an angel who said the following words:

"I will visit you again next year and your wife will then have a son." After this, the Torah tells us that Sara laughed.

Professor Abraham Joshua Heschel said that we learn three things from the angel's statement:

One: Introductory remarks must be brief;

Two: That they must be witty (as it is written that "Sara laughed"), and

Three: That they must be *pregnant* with meaning!

Dear Chief Rabbi Sacks and friends:

Our lecture tonight is called "After Modern Orthodoxy, Then What?" Indeed this is a most important and challenging topic. What is the future of modern-orthodoxy? And to what extent will it be effective in bringing modern Jews closer to Torah and inspiring them to grow in their relationships with God? The title of this lecture is most appropriate. We have to move Modern Orthodoxy beyond its present state. We have to infuse Modern Orthodoxy with a new spirit just as Rabbi Samson

---

[1] Delivered on May 25, 2003 for the David Cardozo Academy.

Raphael Hirsch did when he founded the movement in the nineteenth century. It is indeed a time for bold decisions and creative thought.

In our days Modern orthodoxy has fallen victim to staleness and redundancy. While the movement's leaders include many creative and outstanding thinkers, and thus has tremendous potential, modern orthodoxy has yet to inspire, especially in Israel, our people to come back to the *Beit Hamidrash* and to *Shemirat Hamitzvot.*

This indeed is one of the great challenges of religion in general. It must constantly start all anew while staying true to an old road. It was Sören Kierkegaard, the great Danish existentialist, who once observed that religion has to function like a thunderstorm, but often it just invents lightening conductors.

Indeed to be religious is to defy and to dare.

Faith, we must remember, is not a comfortable state of consciousness. It is more like succor in the midst of a dangerous and unceasing conflict.

To be Jewish is bliss, and a continuous adventure. But to live up to this gift, we must make sure that we perform every religious ritual with feeling and sensitivity, each time as if they were entirely new to us. Religion is warfare, a fight against inertia, indolence, and callousness.

The Talmud says that every soldier in the house of David who was sent to the battle-field was asked to write a bill of divorce for his wife so that if he died or was captured by the enemy, his wife would not become an *agunah.*

The great Chassidic sage, the Kotzker Rebbe, once said about this practice that "To be a Jew is to be at war, and whoever hopes to win a battle must first divorce himself from all other interests and external matters."

Indeed the question modern orthodoxy must grapple with is whether its engagement with the modern world, secular studies, science, sociology, philosophy, and psychology are truly part of a deeply religious experience through which one meets the Divine? Or is this engagement with the secular world really a manifestation of other interests that are entirely disconnected from religious beliefs and observance?

A strong commitment to Halacha coupled with an open-mindedness to change where change is really necessary should continue to be a priority for modern orthodoxy. But at the same time the movement's leaders must understand that when change is not necessary, then it is necessary *not* to change.

May God grant the Modern Orthodox world this wisdom.

51

Emerging Cracks: The State of Jewish Education Today[1]

Introducing Rabbi Adin Steinsaltz

Only the High Priest was allowed to enter the Holy of Holies in the Temple in Jerusalem, and only once a year – on Yom Kippur.

But sometimes, even the Holy of Holies needed some repairs. To provide for such an eventuality, King Solomon designed openings in an upper chamber that led down through the ceiling of the Holy of Holies. Workmen were lowered into this most holy space in *"tevot"* (boxes) through the holes in the ceiling. The Talmud relates that the holes were close to the walls and that the boxes were only open on the wall-side so that the workmen "could not feast their eyes on the Holy of Holies."[2]

Interestingly, the chamber above the Holy of Holies was even less accessible than the Holy of Holies itself, for the High Priest entered the Holy of Holies once every year, whereas this upper chamber was entered only once every fifty years in order to see if the room required any repairs.

In Chassidic thought this tradition has profound allegorical significance.

In Hebrew *"tevot"* means both "boxes" and also "words." As such the "words" of Jewish tradition are seen as the means by which one may enter the Holy of Holies within the heart of every Jew, so that we can repair and revive their souls.

Jewish Education is in need of radical repairs. We live in an era in which the Jewish religious imagination seems to be exhausted. We no

---

[1] Delivered on May 12, 2003 for the David Cardozo Academy.
[2] Pesachim 26a.

longer seem to know how to lower ourselves via the *tevot* into the Holy of Holies of our children's hearts.

We have fallen victim to sociological and anthropological approaches, which has led to the vulgarization of Jewish education. We ask whether we Jews are a race, a people, an ethnicity, a religion, a cultural entity, a historic group, or linguistic unit. And yet we fail to ask the most important questions: Who are we morally? Who are we spiritually? What do we owe the world, and what is our mission here? We may be busy trying to repair Judaism, but we seem to be descending into a temple of secularity.

Jewish education today deals with a great amount of very interesting information, but we forget that we should be concerned primarily with *transformation.* Jewish Tradition teaches us that the experience of walking around within the Temple inspired people to spiritually metamorphosize. People were astonished by the many miracles that occurred constantly in the Temple. It was not merely Jewish continuity that the Temple sought to guarantee, but a radical life-altering re-formation of the Jewish soul. The Temple experience nurtured souls to grow wings so that they could fly.

The Temple demonstrated the awesome spiritual power of the Torah, so that man could perceive God everywhere, like the Chassidic Rebbe who walked in the forest because he wanted to watch the tall swaying trees *"davening Shemoneh Esrei."*[3]

Proper Jewish education should be just like a work of art that introduces us to our most cherished thoughts and emotions. It must protest against stagnancy and redundancy. *It is boring unless it surprises us!* Jewish educators must strive to remember that a thought can be a prison for the mind if it does not invoke an outburst of amazement.

---

[3] Praying the "18 benedictions" while standing in great concentration, often accompanied by swinging of the upper body. I heard this story in the name of Rabbi Abraham Joshua Heschel *z"l.*

52

Halachic Limits to Halacha:
Rabbinical Authority in the Modern Era[1]

Introducing Professor Dov Frimer

Never before has Halacha been so challenged as it is in our days, especially in Israel.

For nearly two thousand years, Jews lived under foreign rule and were thus able to play the role of what I call "comfortable spectators." They stood on the side while their host nations struggled with legal problems and moral crises. Throughout history these nations frequently looked for ways to increase the efficacy of their systems of government. So too, they often changed their positions about proper standards of morality.

Probably on more than a few occasions, Jewish citizens smiled when they saw how their host countries failed to enact and abide by sensible and ethical principles of justice. Jews saw themselves as wise men who, if the rulers of nations would only ask, could explain how to run things with much greater success.

True, many Jewish individuals served as advisors and ministers in many a gentile government, but *as a nation* the Jews never (while in exile) participated in operating a government. Under such circumstances it was relatively easy to criticize, and to convince oneself of one's vastly superior wisdom. We were sure that if given the opportunity, we would do much better. We did not have a country of our own, and so we were able to hold on to our convictions without ever having to prove ourselves. This was indeed one of the very few luxuries granted to us in exile. We

---

[1] Delivered on March 3, 2003 for the David Cardozo Academy.

could easily criticize and smile while the gentile world struggled. We were comfortable spectators.

Since we returned to our homeland, everything changed. Now we are no longer onlookers. Suddenly we became responsible for running a nation. Suddenly we were asked to create a legal system for our new state. Suddenly we had to do it for ourselves, and others were put in the position to smile from a distance.

To run a secular, but Jewish, country is an almost impossible task. The idea alone is a contradiction in terms. Secular, but Jewish? The difficulties come from all sides, but one of the major obstacles no doubt arises from the fact that the purpose of secular law differs from that of Jewish Law.

Two great Jewish thinkers, living in two totally different worlds, made this point in an almost identical way. One was Rabbi Eliyahu Eliezer Dessler, the famous *mashgiach ruchani*, spiritual leader, of the Ponevezh Yeshiva in Bnei Brak, Israel, and the other was Professor Moshe Silberg, deputy member of Israel's Supreme Court.

Both made the following observation:

Secular law is *rights orientated,* while Jewish law is *duty orientated.* While the main point in secular law is to defend and uphold the rights of the citizen, Halacha is a system that constantly emphasizes the moral and religious obligations of each man to his fellow and to his God. We see this philosophical stance in the fact that the Torah never expresses itself in terms of human rights but always in the form of obligations: "Thou shalt... and thou shalt not...."

This automatically creates tension between a modern, secular society and the Jewish ideal. Modern secular society sees its success in terms of making sure that its citizens are happy and financially prosperous. It is in *this* that secular man hopes to find his dignity and his liberty. Not so in Judaism. Judaism sees man's liberty and dignity in terms of his responsibilities. A man is a man, not because he does what he wants to do, but because he does what he *ought* to do.

We could say this a little differently. Secular law's major task is to guarantee and uphold the concept of civilization – to make sure that man behaves in a civilized manner. After all, this leads to the greatest levels of comfort and physical satisfaction for the greatest number of people.

But this is not the purpose of Halacha at all. Judaism is not interested in the civilized man per se. Judaism is *the art of surpassing civilization*. Judaism is interested in creating *tzaddikim*, righteous people. Its most central word is *kedusha*, holiness. Judaism sets man the task of becoming a holy being, not merely civilized.

I believe that this philosophical rift lies at the root of the conflict between the religious vision for the State of Israel and the secular one. Is it at all possible to create an equilibrium between these two competing value systems? Or are they mutually exclusive? Rights vs. Obligations. *Kedusha* vs. Prosperity.

Can Halacha somehow function within a secular system that does not buy into its overall ideology? Does the Jewish Tradition provide guidance on how to introduce Halacha into a secular system in such a way that the latter slowly but surely incorporates more and more of its duty and *kedusha*-orientated ideology?

Above all: Does Halacha have a framework for initiating a step-by-step healing process that will bring its original ideology of *kedusha* back to the center of Jewish life?

These are the issues with which future generations of Jewish thinkers and Halachic authorities will have to grapple. Their success will require courage, creativity, and most of all, an unusual amount of *Yirat Shamayim* – fear of Heaven.

Rabbi Bezalel Rakov *z"l* of Gateshead – Eulogy

"Death is the supreme festival on the road to freedom."[1]

It is with great pain that I write about the demise of one of the great rabbinical figures of our generation, Rabbi Bezalel Rakov *z"l* who headed a small settlement of deeply religious Jews in the city of Gateshead in the north of England.

Gateshead's Jewish Community is the most famous bastion of Torah learning in Europe. Some of the greatest Jewish leaders and rabbis were educated in this poor little town with its venerable yeshiva and numerous institutions of Jewish learning. Only to those who really searched did it reveal its spiritual richness and piety.

My wife and I had the honor of living in Gateshead for many years before returning to Holland and then later settling in Jerusalem. While residing there, Rabbi Rakov helped me give birth to, and nurtured, my Jewish aspirations.

As one of the few "baalei teshuva"[2] (I believe there were another two) among the hundreds and hundreds of ultra-orthodox young Jews learning in Gateshead Yeshiva, I had the opportunity to become well-acquainted with Rabbi Rakov on numerous visits to his home. Coming from a secular background, I had many philosophical questions and issues with Halacha with which no one had ever confronted him before. Yet, it was with remarkable ease that he related to my unique situation – as if he penetrated to the depths of my life's challenges in a matter of

---

[1] Dietrich Bonhoeffer, *Miscellaneous Thoughts, Letters and Papers from Prison*, 1953.

[2] Returnees to Judaism

moments. I still remember his distinguished smile and sparkling eyes when he saw me walking into his front room, knowing quite well that I would once more badger him with "impossible" Halachic circumstances and philosophical inquiries. Not once did he fail to help me achieve clarity. Not halachically, and not philosophically.

Who was Rabbi Rakov?

Maimonides, in the introduction to his *Yad Hachazaka* states that Ahiya Hashiloni,[3] who lived during the days of the breakdown of the House of David, studied under Moshe and consequently must have been hundreds of years old. He spanned many generations. God, we are told, kept him alive for so many centuries so that the younger generations would get a glimpse of a person who lived in an era of spiritual genius the likes of which had long vanished. Ahiya Hashiloni stood as an example of what men could be. He demonstrated the stature of those who handed the tradition down to us, who lived in a different, more elevated, realm of existence.

So was Rabbi Rakov. He was the soul of an ancient generation of rabbinical figures planted in the present. He was the Ahiya Hashiloni who connected his students to different worlds and showed us what a real Jew is supposed to be, and what it meant to have rabbinic dignity. As a teacher of God's word, a vestige of an ancient era, a remnant of the scribes of the past, he inspired us with his impeccable conduct in every moment, his shyness, his wisdom, and his constant desire to stay in the background while gently revealing his mastery in this small but very strong Jewish community, which housed world-renowned rabbinical figures from Eastern Europe.

Rabbi Rakov lived in the holy realms of the universe and thus saw the Divinity invested in every being. He daily demonstrated to his students the ideal relationship between God and Man.

Not only did he rely on God, but it was as clear as the sun that God relied on him. Not only did he represent the best of what a man of

---

[3] See *Bava Batra* 121b and *Sota* 13a

faith can be, but he also justified God's faith in man. It was his rabbinical royalty and unprecedented integrity, which made us all stand in awe of him. Indeed he was the ideal hareidi, ultra-orthodox Rabbi, who inspired a certain young man with a ponytail who was traveling through the country. One day this boy appeared at Rabbi Rakov's front door. The rabbi invited him over for Shabbat, and ended up giving him his father's *teffilin* under the condition that he would wear them throughout his life.

His loyalty to all of us sustained our faith. In fact he taught us to have faith in faithfulness. He taught us that faith in the living God was not easily attained and that one needed to be a little embarrassed by living in His presence. While men can try to sever themselves from God, Rabbi Rakov proved that there was no escape from the love of His Law.

With his demise, the world has lost a great human being, but Heaven has gained more beauty. There they are no doubt celebrating his arrival and his freedom from physical constraints. On earth we should remember the example he set and try to become authentic Jews – men of moderation, deeply religious, with an ongoing love for every Jew whatever his background. Like Rabbi Rakov, we should strive to be wholly committed to the word of God. This indeed is the hareidi Jew par excellence!

I thank the Holy One, blessed be He, that I had the merit to know him.

May his memory be blessed.

About the Author

Rabbi Dr. Nathan Lopes Cardozo is a world renowned thinker, lecturer and ambassador for Judaism and the Jewish people. He is known for his original insights into how authentic Judaism is able to show new ways in which to respond to the spiritual and intellectual challenges of modernity. A prolific author, Rabbi Lopes Cardozo's books and essays are read by laymen, Rabbis and academicians throughout the Jewish and non-Jewish world. He is a sought-after lecturer on Judaism and Israel at numerous institutions of higher academic learning, including Jewish Study programs at leading Universities, Religious Academies and Rabbinical Colleges. He is the founder and Dean of the David Cardozo Academy in Jerusalem which is dedicated to educating a new generation of Rabbis, teachers, and Jewish thinkers based on his captivating philosophy.

Rabbi Lopes Cardozo pens a weekly "Thought to Ponder" which may be subscribed to through the website www.cardozoschool.org and is a distinguished member the Spanish Portuguese Community of Amsterdam. He received his rabbinical degree from Gateshead Talmudic College in England and lives with his wife, children and grandchildren in Jerusalem.

Publication of this book was assisted by the
The David Cardozo Academy
Machon Ohr Aaron
7 Cassuto Street
Jerusalem 96433 Israel
Tel: 972 2 6524053 Fax: 972 2 6517417
Email: cacademy@012.net.il
www.cardozoschool.org